Tea and Pomegranates

Also by Nazneen Sheikh

NOVELS

Ice Bangles

Chopin People

YOUNG ADULT

Camels Can Make You Homesick and Other Stories

Heartbreak High

Lucy (Degrassi series)

A Memoir of Food, Family and Kashmir

Tea and Pomegranates

Nazneen Sheikh

PENGUIN
CANADA

PENGUIN CANADA

Published by the Penguin Group

Penguin Group (Canada), 90 Eglinton Avenue East, Suite 700, Toronto, Ontario, Canada
M4P 2Y3 (a division of Pearson Penguin Canada Inc.)

Penguin Group (USA) Inc., 375 Hudson Street, New York, New York 10014, U.S.A.
Penguin Books Ltd, 80 Strand, London WC2R 0RL, England
Penguin Ireland, 25 St Stephen's Green, Dublin 2, Ireland (a division of Penguin Books Ltd)
Penguin Group (Australia), 250 Camberwell Road, Camberwell, Victoria 3124, Australia
(a division of Pearson Australia Group Pty Ltd)
Penguin Books India Pvt Ltd, 11 Community Centre, Panchsheel Park, New Delhi – 110 017,
India
Penguin Group (NZ), cnr Airborne and Rosedale Roads, Albany, Auckland 1310, New Zealand
(a division of Pearson New Zealand Ltd)
Penguin Books (South Africa) (Pty) Ltd, 24 Sturdee Avenue, Rosebank, Johannesburg 2196,
South Africa

Penguin Books Ltd, Registered Offices: 80 Strand, London WC2R 0RL, England

First published 2005

1 2 3 4 5 6 7 8 9 10 (RRD)

LIBRARY AND ARCHIVES CANADA CATALOGUING IN PUBLICATION

Sheikh, Nazneen
Tea and pomegranates : a memoir of food, family and Kashmir / Nazneen Sheikh.

ISBN 0-14-301779-9

1. Sheikh, Nazneen. 2. Pakistani Canadians—Food—Azad Kashmir.
3. Cookery, Pakistani. 4. Pakistani Canadians—Biography. I. Title.

TX649.S55A3 2005   641.595491'3   C2005-903164-6

Visit the Penguin Group (Canada) website at **www.penguin.ca**

For Malka

Contents

❧

❧

❧

Acknowledgments

Sometimes this Kashmiri houseboat, carrying food, family history and traces of a Mughal dream, lost an oar, ran into a sandbank or rocked perilously in the wake of a storm. On these occasions a band of trusty mariners shifted the weight to the centre and pretended they had not seen the compass being hurled overboard. For this I am filled with gratitude and profound respect.

I wish to thank my Kashmiri clan residing in Pakistan and elsewhere for providing the inspiration for the book. My mother, Dilafroze, for beaming out love from Lahore. Cloudland Guru M for suggesting that I could write this book and for being there at the beginning, middle and end. Malka Green for nurturing mythical places in the heart. Sharon Cohen, my brilliant solicitor, for reminding Canadian superior court judges that writers need to eat so they can write about eating! Federico Alodi for his timely accusations and unbridled appetite. My agent, David Lavin, for representing me so ably. My editor, Susan Folkins, for being "the Eagle." The production team of Penguin Canada, Eliza Marciniak and copy editor Marcia Miron, for displaying sensitivity and enhancing the text. Jeanot Jahangir Malik for pampering me in Lahore. My beloved cousins Tahir, Tayab, Salman and Shujat for assisting in family research. Dr. Steven Connell for taking care of the soul. Consuelo Jackman for being wildly enthusiastic about coming for dinner. My muses, Eva Luna and Kiran Sihra, for ordering the best pizza in town. Jie Jalal Matar for his matchless ability to present *nazrana* on every encounter and for being thoroughly Mughal at heart. Andrew Hubert Willman for ensuring that a steady supply of chocolate reached the Endhouse. Peter Ralphs for sending music to write by. Aneesudin Ahmad, Pakistan's ambassador to France and his wife, la begum, for providing two croissants for breakfast in Paris. Finally, to Superman, who made peach and apricot jam, marinated roasted red peppers, lamb couscous and Moroccan tomatoes for me and sliced a cucumber in my kitchen so that it unfurled like a flower in the palm of his hand. Salut!

Introduction

As a child growing up in Kashmir and Pakistan, I spent the first twenty years of my life with people who regarded cooking and eating as one of the great pleasures of life. The delicious food they served convinced me they were right. Some of my relatives still tease me that as a toddler I could be fed anything, and my animated response to favoured foods soared above the excitement of receiving a toy. My childhood left me with a lifelong obsession with food, as well as an endless fascination with members of my family. I often felt that they could easily have been characters in the books I devoured in my childhood, whose romantic and adventurous lives were embellished by the stunning cuisine they effortlessly presented.

In adulthood my boundaries were extended and I made a home in Canada, but I kept returning in my mind to the foods of my childhood. I wanted to preserve the full pageantry of my aging relatives' cuisine and bring to life their cultural heritage, tied to the political history of two neighbouring nations. I hoped this history of Kashmiri food would be a consolation for members of my baroque family, who had lost a homeland during the Partition of India in 1947. This loss, worn as a badge of courage, had a way of disappearing when food was brought to the table.

I was born in Kashmir and raised in Pakistan, where I had many relatives sprinkled throughout the country. Yet throughout my childhood, the history of the nation I lived in and my Kashmiri ancestry made me feel as though I had been separated from a twin at birth. There were two Kashmirs, my parents would tell me. One existed in Pakistan and was thought to be the fake one, while the other, the real Kashmir, where I had been born, was part of India. Some of our relatives had stayed behind in India-controlled Kashmir, but because my parents had taken part in the struggle for independence from Britain and India, our family moved to Pakistan. Still, as a child I could not fully understand why they had left the real Kashmir behind.

India was to be divided into two nations. It was a country with a vast population of Hindus and comparatively fewer Muslims. Indian provinces with Muslim populations would form the new nation of Pakistan, of which the state of Kashmir was to be an integral part. Somewhere amid the turmoil of the civil war, Kashmir was lost. My family was among those Kashmiris who felt that the move to Pakistan was temporary and one day they would return to the town of Srinagar, where they belonged. Instead, the borders of both countries were immediately sealed, and my family could not look back.

This is my reason for writing *Tea and Pomegranates:* the food served by my family refused to acknowledge boundaries. It was infused with magical ingredients and flavoured with yearning, love, art and history. In their cooking, my family followed the traditions of one of the grand cuisines of the world, Mughal cuisine. The Mughals, descendants of four central Asian peoples—Mongols, Persians, Afghans and Turks—ruled India and gave birth to my ancestors generations ago.

The Mughal empire was consumed by a passion for creating beauty and heightening sensual pleasure. Cuisine, art, architecture, philosophy and poetry flourished under the rule of avowed patrons of the arts. Imperial libraries, such as the one built by Emperor Akbar; fountains, gardens and poetry recitation pavilions created by Emperor Jahangir; and architectural wonders like the Monument of Love, also known as the Taj Mahal, commissioned by Emperor Shah Jehan, bear testimony to this glut of aestheticism that depleted treasuries and eventually resulted in the demise of the empire.

It was the state of Kashmir, perched on the northern tip of India, that made contact with Persian civilization via the Silk Route in the fourteenth century. Kashmiris were the first to enhance their culture by experimenting with outside influences. Although Turkey, Afghanistan, Iran and Mongolia today are sovereign nations, for two centuries they mingled to create a people whose culinary legacy has been curiously underemphasized in South Asian cuisine.

Turkish and Persian influences flavoured Mughal cuisine with nuts, dried seeds of fruits, herbs and lighter-tasting spices like cumin and coriander. Convention dictated that all seasoning was to be tasted individually. Most of the sauces were yogourt, cardamom and saffron based, and cayenne, which tends to numb the palate to other flavours, was used moderately. However, Mughal chefs also used cayenne to prevent bacteria from forming in certain foods. In the unusual Hyderabadi cuisine, almost a subspecialty of the grand Mughal cuisine, with a heavy emphasis on lime, tamarind and citric sauces, chilies were treated as vegetables. They were coated with yogourt and salt and dried in the sun, then fried and served with meals as condiments. Fresh green chilies also were served as a distinct entree, combined with tamarind and ground sesame paste to neutralize the fiery taste and bulk the sauce.

While Mughal cuisine wildly embraced every element that romanced the palate, Indian cuisine later was sharply divided. The Hindus, largely vegetarian, revered the cow and considered it a deity. The Muslims, who were meat-eaters, slaughtered the animal and consumed its flesh. In the Hindu Brahman priestly hierarchy, food cooked by a member of a lower caste was unacceptable. Muslims, on the other hand, served and accepted food cooked by anyone. Even garlic and onions, considered heating agents, were forbidden to the Hindus. A century after the fall of the Mughal empire, the partition of India appeared to be a logical solution.

The Mughal empire of fifteenth-century India was based within shifting geographical boundaries. Yet in the history of an assimilated cuisine, Kashmiri food resisted fusing with others and retained a magical allure. It was as though the people who prepared and ate this cuisine remained authentic Mughals long after the demise of the empire.

In Pakistan, where I grew up, varying provincial cuisines overshadowed Kashmiri cuisine, and *wazas*, or Kashmiri banquet chefs, were not easy to find. These chefs held a unique place in their culture. They refused to permit others to serve the food they had cooked, even though meals had a minimum of eleven courses. They also insisted on using only freshly slaughtered meat.

Artists of both countries drew inspiration from the Mughal era, depicting Mughal costumes, converting poetry into film lyrics and reproducing their cuisine and social etiquette. To me, Mughal cuisine assumed the guise of a haunting ideal, and eating a meal prepared by a Kashmiri waza was a rare and unforgettable experience. In the same way, I viewed my mother separating strands of saffron with her fingertips or my grandmother carefully slicing lotus roots as symbols of this romantic history.

The key to my family culinary history rests in the spirit of Dil-Aram, my maternal grandmother. Although my mother and her seven siblings were awe-inspiring cooks, I am compelled to return time and again to my grand-mother's kitchen, where magical food and a dramatic family history were stored side by side. As a child, I was permitted to enter, linger and hide in this kitchen, which to me assumed the dimensions of Ali Baba's cave. My fascination with my grandmother was fuelled by her atti-tude to cooking. Precision, inventiveness and a desire to always give pleasure were her innate characteristics. There was no room for error, and preparing a meal was a full-scale production, in which colour, texture and design played significant roles. Cooking is sorcery, she taught me—a meal could make one break into verse, weep copiously or even dance between courses.

When I left Pakistan and settled in Canada, I was finally able to understand my parents' dilemma of losing a homeland, but I also came to realize that culture has movement. My nostalgia for the country of my child-hood rests in my memories of food. When I cook, I know that if both the palate and the imagination are engaged, then I have served an excellent meal. Food can be traced in the outlines of stunning architecture, in poetic imagery, in the spun gold of brocades or even in acts of war. Above all, food is the greatest expression of love and contentment.

The most astounding thing about cuisine is that it is portable: any meal can be prepared anywhere at any time. While living in a remote village in Italy during a writing sabbatical, I invited my only friend, the owner of the local store, to my hilltop villa for dinner. I cooked for her my mother's saffron-almond chicken. I spent hours pounding whole spices with a small hammer I found in a toolkit. I shed tears over my inability to find a substitute for basmati rice, hurled invective at the short-grained Italian arborio variety and finally consoled myself by plundering the hill-side for poppies for the table. My guest looked deep into my eyes and declared that I was in fact a Roman. I told her that she was a Mughal because she came bearing wine from her village, Ortuccio, in Abruzzi, and freshly baked biscuits. There are few creative endeavours that can match the potential of cooking for giving and receiving pleasure.

After arriving in North America, I found the people equally food obsessed. Surprisingly, they too expressed a yearning—for flavours and traditions lost, or new frontiers sought. Holistic, naturopathic and weight loss—oriented cookbooks leapt off the shelves of book-stores. Television shows featured people slicing and folding after the prevailing fashion of the day. The visual imagery was stunning, but I could not identify with these cuisine "fashionistas," and I regularly sent food back in restaurants with messages for the chefs. I was looking for flavours and textures that displayed both respect and passion. I wanted to see shooting stars, picture pearls hiding in oysters and instantly write a poem upon tasting something superb. What nourished my body had to feed the soul. I even recklessly contemplated writing this book in verse.

Instead, I thought of my large Kashmiri family in Pakistan. Despite the adventures of my own life, I could not conjure a more powerful host of characters. The stack of family photographs resting in a brown envelope in the basement of my Toronto home were more than a fading montage of a family history. Within these photographs were chefs, lovers and magicians, each of whom had cooked dishes that are the most accomplished part of a dazzling repertoire.

The contemporary South Asian cookbooks filled with vibrant colours and artful photography did not single out Kashmiri Mughal cuisine and its dynamic evolution. My beloved relatives were blessed with the art of cooking through memory. Not only did they shower me with affection, they also passed this legacy to me. I could sit continents away in my Canadian kitchen and duplicate their cooking techniques. Yet sometimes an elusive ingredient would alter the response of the palate. On those occasions I knew that my relatives had flavoured the food I had eaten with their personalities. I felt that presenting their personal histories and their recipes and allowing them to cook at all hours and on all occasions would be like throwing a Mughal banquet. And so I now request the pleasure of the company of guests at the table of a Kashmiri family for breakfast, lunch and dinner.

Tea and Pomegranates

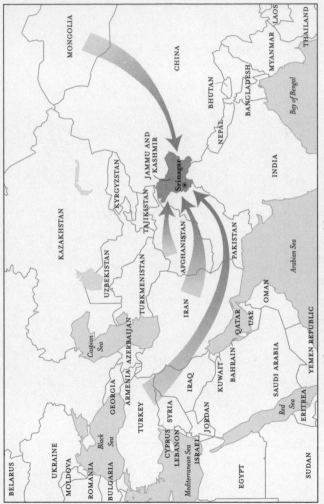

CULINARY INFLUENCES ON MUGHAL CUISINE

1

A Handful of Green Tea Leaves

⋙

My grandmother poured the pink tea from the samovar into a cup. I watched the straight line of her black eyebrows crease as she shredded a spiral of gossamer-thin pastry into the tea. Flakes of gold *bakarkhani* danced on the surface then formed a mouth-watering lump at the bottom. I was ten years old, and this was my first exposure to a typical Kashmiri breakfast. This was also my first visit to my grandmother's home, in a town called Rawalpindi in Pakistan.

She slid the cup toward me across the white table-cloth. As I blew on the surface, my grandmother's kohl-rimmed eyes widened, and a smile tugged at her lips. She leaned forward and exhaled deeply over the cup, subtly reminding me to modify my exuberant breathing, while acknowledging that everything served at her table was boiling hot.

With my first sip, I felt as though I were being pummelled by a wave and accidentally swallowing seawater, but what lingered on my palate was curiously pleasant. My grandmother told me that the rose-coloured liquid had been flavoured with salt. As I sipped the tea and spooned up the drowned pastry at record speed, she poured another cup and handed me another pastry. She alerted me to the sound of pastry snapping, in her seamless fashion imparting a lesson in detecting freshness. I wondered if this was a breakfast made specially for me and hoped that it would replace the beige-coloured milk and Ovaltine I was used to drinking at tea time.

❦

The dark green Kashmiri tea leaves resemble the oolong tea of China. As Kashmir borders China, it was assumed that the Silk Route merchants had imported this green tea, until 1773, when the British East India Trading Company found indigenous tea bushes in the hillsides of Darjeeling, Assam and Nilgri.

Kashmiri tea tastes unlike any other because of the way it is brewed. The leaves are brewed with milk, which softens the bite of tannin and tinges the liquid pale pink. The simmering milk also brings cream to the surface, soothing the palate and banishing any disagreeableness.

From my grandmother, I learned that the ratio of tea to water was critical, as was the quality of fresh milk that would give not the first, but the second cream. Any digression from the formula evoked a characteristic response from her. Rather than openly expressing disdain, she widened her eyes until grey light shot through her topaz-coloured irises, drawing back from the impostor tea with movements as stylized as those of a kabuki performer. This inability to accept lack of perfection hinted at her Mughal temperament—it was as though she had directly inherited the precision with which her ancestors laid out a geometric design or a blueprint for conquest.

My grandmother's rejection of carelessly prepared food and drink was theatrically duplicated by three generations of my clan. To my grandmother, the desire to savour a well-prepared meal not only heightened the pleasure of anticipation, but also placed responsibility in the hands of the person cooking. Preparing and consuming food was a life-sustaining ritual that depended on more than mere ingredients, for there was also the emotional palette to consider. Respect, appreciation, consolation and even seduction sprang from what others would consider simply a meal.

That morning, with my parents, my brother, Shahid, and my elder sister, Mahjabin, yet to arrive at the table for breakfast, my grandmother sat attentively as I ate, making me feel that keeping me company was a pleasure for her. On the wall of the simple white-washed dining room, a portrait of my bearded and heavily jowled grandfather watched over us. This was the man whose personal mythology was so overwhelming that it threatened to overshadow the living presence of my grandmother. I almost expected him to jump out of the sepia-toned photograph and demand why *kulchas,* hard, round flour-and-soda biscuits studded with sesame seeds, had not been served with Kashmiri tea. My grandmother told me he was a purist at heart, yet she had served the more refined pastry to indulge me. I felt her indulgence was a sign of favour that was to be a special secret between us.

My grandmother sat at the table with a regal posture, like a queen who had stepped from the pages of a fairy tale. She was a slender woman with a sharp aquiline nose, high cheekbones, fine lips and multihued topaz eyes—pure Kashmiri features in which the Mongol and the Persian were entwined, while my grandfather had the dark flashing eyes, fleshy nose and sensual mouth of the Turks and Afghans. She wore her dark hair, sprinkled with silvery strands, gathered into a braid or a tightly coiled chignon at the nape of her neck. In her home her hair was uncovered, but when she went out she would drape a length of georgette over her head. In a country where women wore sandals in the summer, she wore fine socks and soft-soled leather pumps. She dressed in soft pastels—whites, sky blues and on the rare occasion a pale violet—and her vivid beauty was unadorned by any jewellery or cosmetics.

Her resilience and grace gave her a particular style that I would secretly try to mimic. When she spoke, she articulated words majestically, but when amused, she would giggle like a young girl. At those moments, I forgot that she was a grandmother.

Seeing that I had finished my breakfast, she rose in a flutter of grey crepe garments, and I followed her toward the kitchen. Entering the dimly lit room, I felt her pull me close to her. She informed me that the samovar was being cleaned, and I was to observe this ritual because when I grew up I would have to know how to do this in my own home.

My grandmother's samovar was a large jug-shaped container of embossed silver metal with a pouring spout on one end and a handle on the other. Her kitchen helper, a young man with close-cropped hair, lifted the lid, tilting the samovar so a stream of fiery coals descended from the latticework base and through the central column into the open fire of the stove. He allowed the samovar to cool for a few minutes, then scrubbed the inner chamber. Finally, he placed it on a small stone disc on a shelf for the next morning, when the pink tea would be brewed for breakfast.

While the samovar was being cleaned, my grandmother gently recited a history lesson. I could hear the hoofbeats of Mongolian ponies cantering across the vast Gobi Desert as they headed toward the Hindu Kush Mountains and the Karakorum range, which guarded the frontiers of India. The Mongolians, a migratory people, conducted their entire span of existence in motion. Eating and cooking utensils had to be designed for travel, and so they designed the exquisitely logical samovar, with a chamber for fuel and a separate chamber for brewing liquid both in one container. Later, the samovar would be imported into Russia and other parts of Europe. In southern Asia it was decorated with regional craftsmanship and motifs. The Turks and Persians added glittering discs of enamel featuring detailed motifs and intricate sets of spigots. Silver was used only as a plating device, while the favoured metal was copper.

My first exposure, years ago, to Kashmiri tea in my grandmother's home was tinged with mystery. I left the kitchen and walked into the open courtyard of her home. A flood of sunlight cascaded down, and for a moment the green kitchen door across the courtyard shimmered like a mirage. Even the three-storey house looping over the courtyard tilted at surreal angles. I was instantly catapulted into an image from my earlier childhood. I was seated in a tiny alcove beneath a wooden structure. Seated next to me was a little boy who was my playmate. We were both holding a little metal bowl, which was filled with fresh green peas sprinkled with sugar. It was apparent that the peas had been given to us by an adult, but sugar was a contraband item, which led to our hiding.

I felt upon recovering this memory that I had just been tapped on the shoulder by a ghost. It was the ghost of Bashirabad, my grandparents' house in Srinagar. The little alcove was underneath the bottom step of the staircase in that home, and the little boy was my first cousin. As the image receded, I had no knowledge that a country had been divided and a homeland lost, or that my enthralling grandmother had lost every privilege to which she had been accustomed.

❦

Despite the reshaping of their lives by civil war, my grandparents' life together, in a town called Srinagar in the state of Kashmir, had been a charmed one. At the age of sixteen, in the early 1900s, my grandmother, whose name then was Zuun, consented to marry my grandfather, Khan Sahib Sirajud-din Ahmad Dar. He was a widower in his early thirties, with five children, a claim to an ancestral village and a title; he was also fluent in four languages and enjoyed a reputation as a literary scholar, poet and gourmand. Zuun was the flower he transformed into Dil-Aram, meaning "heart's ease," for he felt this name did more justice to her beauty.

Without a dent to her composure, she lived up to her name. She bore him another eight children, took lessons in English and catered to every whim of her charismatic yet autocratic husband. Throughout her life, she remained passionately in love with him and his ideals.

This willingness to be mentored by an older husband in both domestic and social matters without sacrificing her individuality set her apart from the conventions of her time. Indian wives of that era were raised to be deferential to their husbands and were not necessarily active companions. Yet despite a brood of children, Dil-Aram and Siraj shared time alone together. He educated her about his greatest passion, poetry, and she kept his notebooks, crammed with poetry, safe after he died.

In Srinagar, my grandparents lived in a rambling wooden house with bay windows and sweeping verandas, which my grandfather called "Bashirabad" after his eldest son, Bashir, from his first marriage. It was a patriarchal gesture designed to ensure continuity.

Tacked on the wall in the kitchen of this house was a recipe for lamb pulao. Many years later, my youngest uncle revealed to me the source of the recipe. During the early 1940s, in pre-Partition India, a renowned chef,

Baba Rorha, came from Lucknow to visit Srinagar. My grandfather dragooned the chef into preparing this dish so the recipe could be recorded for his young bride, Dil-Aram. The magical ingredient was a pink shallot, called *praan,* added to the lamb stock. In a home stocked with a library of first editions, rare carpets and a collection of hunting rifles, this recipe was considered of equal value.

The arrival of another legendary chef to Bashirabad became a memorable family anecdote. The *wazwan* was secretive beyond belief. The young Dil-Aram only saw ingredients sail out of her storeroom as the chef worked in the open-air kitchen in the large back garden, reminiscent of the travelling kitchen brigades of the Mughal armies advancing into India. A visiting uncle of my grandmother, by some stroke of genius, convinced the chef that he would consider it a great honour to sit unobtrusively on a folding camp stool nearby. He carried out his role as the family spy to perfection. Blessed with a superb memory, he passed along a compendium of techniques to his young niece, Dil-Aram. This genius at cooking from memory became a celebrated family trait.

My grandfather, a master of ambience, also assumed a significant role in the proceedings. When the sizzle of caramelizing onions, pounding of spices and clanging of oversized cooking pots reached deafening heights, he headed up to his library to compose a poem for the occasion. Shifting metaphors and even using culinary references, he later regaled the guests with recitations. This twinning of poetry recitations with the consumption of good food is part of Mughal culture. The Mughals believed that to do justice to a meal, one must harmonize sensation; the melody of language prepares the digestive system and stimulates the palate, while firing the imagination.

Although Bashirabad could not compete with the Mughal palaces, with their recitation pavilions surrounded by shallow pools of water, my grandfather's passion for poetry never abated. He expressed a love of Persian poetry and conducted a lifelong correspondence with Muhammad Iqbal, the most important poet of Muslim India in the twentieth century. His own poetry did not go unnoticed. During World War I, the British resident administrator for the state of Kashmir, hard pressed to recruit soldiers for England's war effort, requested that he compose and recite a poem to inspire men to volunteer. This act of poetic virtuosity rested quite simply in an unlined brown notebook.

Even culinary mishaps prompted him to reel off comical limericks, although within the kitchen, catastrophes were dealt with severely. A careless cook who had overcooked rice was asked to consume a plateful of it under my grandfather's supervision, in order to be sensitized to appropriate texture. My grandparents considered the food served at Bashirabad as a reflection of their life. The quantity, quality, presentation and ambience created to serve a meal all were as important as an academic examination, reflecting their exacting temperaments.

When their elder children were married at Bashirabad, my grandparents held wedding banquets prepared by legendary wazwans, Kashmiri chefs. The word *waaz* means "cook" in the Kashmiri language, and *waan* means "shop." My grandfather hired the maharajah of Kashmir's premier chef, Bara Ama, to cook the twenty-course banquet. Freshly slaughtered young lamb was pounded so the fibres were transformed into a foamy, sponge-like substance; dishes were scented with cardamom, saffron, black cumin and yogourt. The chef personally served each course to guests seated on tablecloth-covered carpets. People sat in twos to share the large plate filled with steamed basmati rice, on which he heaped delicate portions of each course. To ensure that guests sampled all of the preceding courses and to add suspense, he saved for last the crowning glory, the *gushtaba,* a large foamy meatball. A satiated appetite mid-course was frowned upon; one simply had to be a champion eater, and the ancient Roman practice of regurgitation was unthinkable.

Even during summer vacations, Kashmiri hospitality was never treated lightly, for it was the guests who brought honour to the host simply by their presence.

In the days of my grandparents' life in Srinagar, friends and relatives descended into the bowl-shaped valley of Kashmir in the summer to escape the heat. The favoured spot was lotus-festooned Dal Lake, where the family kept a houseboat, called the *Shikara*. My grandfather carried out lengthy correspondence over the planned vacations, involving many requests for Kashmiri cuisine from devotees who claimed to have dreamt of one particular dish all winter long.

The houseboats were like sumptuous and baroque floating palaces. Wood-panelled bedrooms and living rooms were decorated with Kashmiri carpets and silk tapestry curtains. Hammered copper, filigree silver and glistening papier-mâché objects completed the decor. Linked to the houseboats in an umbilical fashion were kitchen vessels packed with dry provisions, fruits and vegetables, supplemented daily with fresh meat and fish sold on small merchant houseboats.

It was my grandmother's duty to supervise the purchased food provisions based on my grandfather's sensitively concocted menus for the arriving guests. A closeted academic overwhelmed by ink and paper would be transported by the fragrance of fresh apricots and figs. An ailing cousin was to be presented with Kashmiri *yakhni,* a delicate lamb broth garnished with almonds. It was critical that the almonds be young, with the green husks still on them. Houseboat cooks were interviewed, cajoled and convinced that any culinary travesty would mar my grandfather's reputation as the local gourmand.

This theatrical panache of my grandparents left its mark on three generations of the family. Myth making reached absurd proportions. The only cuisine worth indulging in was Kashmiri—every other cuisine in India was an impostor. One Kashmiri apple could perfume a room. The scent of aged basmati rice cooking could waft down an entire street. Fresh Kashmiri kale had the ability to change its flavour seven times. A Kashmiri fig was the size of an adult fist! These were some of the utterances of the kings and queens of food who galloped through my childhood.

❧

Sometimes even a simple object can become a symbol of family history that is passed down to the next generation. In my history, a samovar became a time machine as it travelled through three generations. A copper samovar hammered out in the North-West Frontier town of Peshawar, Pakistan, travelled to my Canadian home. A sentimental gift sent by my father, it sat on the top shelf of my kitchen gathering dust until one day when I broke charcoal briquettes from the barbeque into bits, lit them and placed them with tongs down the central shaft. I brewed tea and served it to two little Canadian girls, my daughters, for whom the terms

Mughal and Kashmir were simply an exotic inconvenience. Yet years later, one of them, who could have doubled for a Mughal princess, autocratically demanded that I give the samovar to her. I was convinced that she had heard the drumbeat of Mongolian horsemen in her university residence, and so I allowed her to carry a minuscule portion of my history away.

The enchanted space of my grandmother's domain, where food combined with familial love became high art, was an even greater gift to me. I had the privilege of being exposed to a family fairy tale of sorts. I felt responsible for preserving this cultural heritage, for I found that the Mughal dream was shrouded in dust and its grand cuisine appropriated, fused and relegated to oblivion. Yet members of my large extended family behaved as though the baroque splendour of the meals they prepared and consumed were simply a way of life. I perceived the dimensions of a much larger tablecloth, where art, history and food became interchangeable.

Many years after that memorable breakfast, when I first discovered that a handful of green tea leaves could be transformed into a rare delicacy called Kashmiri pink tea, I sensed the tapestry of my grandmother's life unfurl before me. It was 1986, and I was standing on the edge of a lake in Srinagar, shadowed by an Indian intelligence officer who thought I had come like my Mughal ancestors to seize the land. On this visit, complete strangers who were related to me treated me like a prodigal child. Their hospitality was unending, and they served me exquisite meals in their modest homes.

My eldest aunt had a samovar that was a metre tall, from which her strapping sons consumed gallons of Kashmiri tea throughout the day. When I asked them about the legendary Bashirabad, they fell silent for a moment. They informed me that the Indian government had appointed a custodian, as many of the heirs to the property lived in Pakistan. Days later, when I insisted on seeing the family home, I had to scale a huge pile of lumber barricading the front of the house. Silently, I walked through the first floor of the abandoned home, resolving never to tell my family about the emotions I experienced. The burden of loss and anger would not replace the gift I intended to bring back to them. It would be enough to say I had visited their home.

Although Bashirabad is lost, my grandmother's history lives in every cup of Kashmiri tea I drink. Offering her recipe is a way to preserve it. Sitting at Dil-Aram's table that morning, and discovering that a handful of green tea leaves could be transformed into a rare delicacy called Kashmiri pink tea, I hoped the lunch that would follow a few hours later would leap out with the same element of surprise. If tea, which I knew to be beige, had turned to pink, I was convinced that she also had the power to alter meats and vegetables from their customary hues.

Pink Tea (Kashmiri Chai)

Kashmiri tea is a loose green tea available in South Asian grocery stores. It is also referred to as gulabi chai—the word *gulabi* means "pink" in Urdu. Chinese oolong tea, a semi-fermented green tea, also can be used in this recipe. As you drink, remember not to exhale too deeply over the cup. It is entirely possible that the spirit of my grandmother Dil-Aram will issue a reprimand.

2 teaspoons Kashmiri tea leaves
1/2 teaspoon baking powder
3 cups water
2 cups milk
1/4 teaspoon salt

In a small metal saucepan, combine the tea leaves, baking powder and 2 cups of the water and bring to a boil. Reduce the heat and simmer for an hour. Strain the reduced fluid and discard the tea leaves. Add the remaining cup of water to the reduced fluid and boil until foam rises to the surface. Whip the liquid with a fork and reduce the heat. Stir in the milk and salt and simmer for 3 to 5 minutes.

Makes 3 to 4 cups.

2

In My Grandmother's Kitchen I Hear the Story of the Lotus

❦

In April, when I was twelve years old, I returned home from school one day to discover that my parents had bought my brother a new bicycle. Seeing the pinprick of jealousy flicker in my eyes, he promptly offered to take me for a ride. It was a precarious trip on a busy Karachi street where we were forbidden to go. This was my devil-may-care brother's compensation for my sense of deprivation. He stopped at a roadside stand to buy me a virulent-blue Popsicle, which we were also forbidden to eat. On the furious ride home, perched behind him on the tiny saddle, I lost one of my shoes. They were new shoes to be worn for parties, and I was not looking forward to my mother's censure.

However, on our return the most astounding news greeted us, and the missing shoe was quickly forgotten. My parents were going abroad for three weeks, and we children would travel by train to stay with our grandmother in Rawalpindi. This would be a much longer visit than the two days we spent with her last time. I raced to my room and found the box where I kept two of my grandmother's letters to my mother, in which she mentioned my name. Among my collection of seashells and hair ribbons in the box, the letters were a talisman of sorts.

The night before the trip, my father heightened our excitement by giving us a short history lesson. Two-thirds into the journey north, just before the city of Lahore in the province of Punjab, the fabled Grand Trunk Road would run beside the train tracks. In 1530, the Afghan king Sher Shah Suri built this road, which he called Gernali Sarak and Sarak-e-Azam, meaning the "emperor's road." Later renamed the Grand Trunk Road by the British, it was twenty-six hundred kilometres long, beginning in Calcutta, moving through Delhi to Pakistan and looping upward to the North-West Frontier province into Kabul, Afghanistan.

Under the Mughals in the sixteenth century, the road became something of a tourist attraction. The Mughals, believing that travel should not diminish comfort, added horse-changing posts, drinking wells, raised minarets, shrubbery and security posts to preserve law and order. Roadside inns offered local produce, freshly slaughtered meat and river fish, and vendors provided hot meals, even cooked to order. Naan, a yeasted flatbread with a puffed-up, crispy crust, was baked in *tandur*, roadside clay ovens fired by wood. Partridge and lamb kekabs also were cooked in the oven, which grilled everything to perfection.

The Mughals had an outstanding knowledge of hydraulics, and they built three bridges along the span of the road. The materials were both indigenously functional and highly decorative. Ceramic tiles with intricate geometric designs were laid over the building materials. In the cities of Lahore and Rawalpindi, the road broadened into heavily tree-lined boulevards, which the British referred to as the "mall." Food stalls were banned in these boulevards, as were horse-drawn carriages. In his novel *Kim,* which was set along this road, Rudyard Kipling referred to the Grand Trunk as "a wonderful spectacle without crowding—green arched, shade flecked, a river of life."

⚜

The next morning, my father held my hand and told me to keep watching the railway tracks. Any minute now the mighty Tezgam, the wonder speed train, would pull into the Karachi railway station. When the train rushed in within seconds of his announcement, the platform burst with activity and sound. The clang of opening metal doors, the shouting of instructions to porters and the hawking supplications of food vendors caused a ripple of excitement through my twelve-year-old frame. I stood amid a cluster of siblings, parents, luggage and the two house domestics who would accompany us on our trip, Nanny and Lasoo.

Although he was older than us, my parents considered Lasoo a child of the family, and they took care to narrate his personal history. In 1947, Lasoo, the teenaged son of a family domestic, played with my siblings and I in our home in Srinagar while his mother worked. The Indian government had imprisoned my father for championing the formation of Pakistan, and my mother waited for him at home. One morning, Indian army officers came to our house. They told my mother that civil war had erupted, and they could not guarantee our safety. My mother had five minutes to gather her family into a jeep, which would convey us to the Pakistan border. Young Lasoo clung to her and begged her not to leave him behind. She made a harrowing decision within seconds, one that would alter the course of his life, and put him in the jeep with her own children. The separation of the two nations and sealing of the borders prevented Lasoo from being sent back. All of my father's subsequent efforts to locate Lasoo's family failed, and he resolved that as long as he lived the boy would have a place in his household.

Even as children we knew that Lasoo possessed a particular magic that could transform him from server to playmate and protector. He could produce a sensational toy or a delicious sandwich of cold lamb and mint sauce at the drop of a hat, and he was a keeper of secrets. Stamped in his lean, angular face was a pair of twinkling eyes that lit up with ongoing amusement at our childhood vagaries. Our mutual delight blunted the dour temperament of our aging nanny. Lasoo could be counted on to play board games with us, while Nanny gathered sections of my hair into stiff braids that stretched my scalp into rigidity.

My father had reserved a private compartment for this voyage, for he was a civil servant, and privileges of this nature were within his scope. Besides our clothing, hampers of food, Thermoses of chilled drinking water and fresh fruit were loaded into the compartment, furnished with two plank-shaped upholstered seats beneath twin sleeping berths. A large ceiling fan revolved overhead, as this was the era before air conditioning.

The overnight journey would take more than twenty-eight hours. My mother had packed a favourite board game, as well as a large zinc tub, for the trip. I had two Enid Blyton books, hard pellets of American bubble

gum and a small paper bag containing a contraband
food item: three oversized wild red almonds. My mother
had forbidden us to eat this fruit because, according to
her, it would result in a sore throat. Yet when sprinkled with salt and black pepper, the acidic flesh was
transformed into a mouth-puckering concoction that
was irresistible. Part of the thrill came from the fact that
I was secretly challenging my mother's theory, which I had
never quite believed. I had also developed a palate for
unusual tastes.

Minutes before the train left, a large block of ice
arrived and was placed in the zinc tub, positioned on
the floor directly beneath the ceiling fan. The air blowing
off the ice would act as a primitive air conditioner. Lasoo
pulled out handfuls of small mangoes from a wicker
basket and placed them on the ice. My mother had
arranged for this ultimate treat, perhaps to distract us
from homesickness.

As the train began to move and the images of our
waving parents receded, the mangoes succeeded in
diverting our attention. The *chussi*, or sucking mango,
packed the same punch as broken segments of a chocolate bar, for it took at least six or seven to make up a
portion. The tiny bright yellow fruit, ten centimetres in
length, could be eaten only one way: by massaging the
skin gently so the flesh dislodged from the fibrous mesh,
then opening a small hole at the top and sucking up

the juice, followed by the flesh. My fastidious father had dubbed it the "bathroom fruit," as the spectacle of juice dribbling from chins and bits of vigorously sucked fruit flying in all directions made him think immediately of soap, water and containment. My mother, on the other hand, had confidently chosen our favourite treat to beguile and console us.

The chussi is among the more than thirty varieties of natural and hybrid mangoes found in the country. Mangoes are not only eaten as a fruit, but are preserved in oils and served as condiments. They are dried and ground into a fine powder, which is used as seasoning for vegetables. This tart seasoning, called *amchur,* is distinguished from lime and tamarind by its slightly smoky flavour. Unripe green mangoes ground with coriander and green chilies make a chutney that complements almost any dish. Mango pickles include both the pit and the fruit, which take months to soften.

Mughals showed their partiality for the fruit by reproducing it in their fabric designs. The shape of the mango, also known as the paisley in Western cultures, was first reproduced on imperial looms according to the dictates of Empress Nur Jehan, the only Mughal empress whose name was hammered on coins. A consummate politician and lavish patron of the arts, she was also a fashion icon of her time and redesigned her husband's wardrobe and those of his courtiers. Her inspiration on this occasion went no further than the fruit bowl presented to her. Under her direction, court artisans experimented with the mango's shape, giving rise to the elongated paisley. Woven with silk and gold thread into silk and wool fabrics, the paisley became a classic oriental pattern. Centuries later, the fabric mills of Britain reproduced the motif, and it is still popular today.

The first hour of travel left me with a powerful life-long association of train journeys with mangoes. I consumed the sweet fruit while sitting in the prized window seat, a book glued to my lap. When I finished a mango I would lean out the open window, and as the furious wind tore the ribbons from my braided hair, hurl the pits outside, convinced that within days mango trees would line the train tracks.

My brother, Shahid, who had a legendary streak of hooliganism that rarely surfaced in the presence of my parents, demolished thirteen mangoes at breakneck speed. My sister, Mahjabin, and I, terrified that he would transform the pits into an assault weapon, sought immediate protection from the watchful Lasoo. The mango fest was expediently halted, and my brother was reminded that lunch had yet to be served. Our two tiffin carriers, metal stacking containers, were filled with cooked food. But the fruit sugar racing through our systems temporarily dampened our enthusiasm.

While a changing landscape sped beside the train and stations with unfamiliar names flew by, I found my concentration shifting from the story I was reading of two little English schoolgirls. Still miles away from the Grand Trunk Road, I looked out the window repeatedly. Somewhere in the recesses of my imagination lay the hope that a Mughal procession complete with elephants and prancing horses would appear, and I would be the first to see it.

When the tablecloth was thrown over our makeshift lunch table of two square suitcases, my mother's spirit cocooned us. Chicken roasted in saffron and coated with gleaming strands of caramelized onions, a circular pile of clarified butter—infused parathas accompanied by coriander chutney, and a tub of cucumber and tomato wedges sprinkled with vinegar and coarsely ground black pepper were manna from a familiar heaven. As we ate picnic style on enamelled plates, the metronome-like precision of the train's furiously churning wheels induced a hypnotic languor. I fell asleep, waking on the edge of an evening that rapidly shifted to dusk and then to a black night, when all visibility outside ended. The Grand Trunk Road travelled beside us unseen until we reached our destination the next morning.

At the station, Lasoo flagged down a wild-eyed driver, who lashed our suitcases to the hood of his small grey taxi and promptly ignored Lasoo's requests to drive slowly. In an attempt to raise the fare, the taxi driver hurtled through the teeming bazaars, where collision with buses and horse-drawn tongas seemed inches away. When we reached our grandmother's house, we tumbled out of the taxi with great relief.

It was a familiar destination, but I was a few years older on this visit and knew more about the home, which my family often referred to by its address: H196 Murree Road, Rawalpindi. My grandmother's land claims for property left in Kashmir, now part of India, had been settled in arbitrary haste by the government of Pakistan. This process and my grandmother's refusal to contemplate moving to the home she deserved were a source of great distress for my father. The gracious wooden and rambling Bashirabad in Srinagar had been replaced with a four-storey brick structure of the older *haveli* type, situated at the end of a narrow lane. The heavy wooden front door opened up to a central courtyard, around which spiralled the rooms, the kitchen, living room and dining room on the ground floor and the bedrooms upstairs.

Racing into the courtyard, I was swept into a fierce embrace by my grandmother and smothered in the sky-blue silk of her garments. Her hair was gathered in a shiny braid, and an indiscernible fragrance rose from her, which I later learned was the small cardamom pod tucked in her cheek that she used as a natural breath freshener. She examined me carefully as though I were a piece of fruit that could be hiding a bruise, stroked my hair, and told me that I was growing taller and must walk erectly. With a mischievous glint in her eyes, she then stated that there was a box of "kareem rolls" in the kitchen, deliberately pulling out an extra first syllable in the word "cream." I was torn by a maddening etiquette instilled by my mother not to dash off for food, so I beamed my appreciation but remained still. However, the little push between my shoulders was signal enough that I was free to make the unseemly dash.

My grandmother had ordered the puff-pastry horns, filled with whipped cream, from a local bakery, as a way of paying deference to my anglicized upbringing a thousand miles away in Karachi. It also had to do with the legacy of French and British cooks in occupied India of another era and my grandmother's appreciation for the skilful cooking of any culture. However, little did we both know at the time that it was the food simmering in her cooking pots, providing the history of a family and culture, that I would try to re-create in my Canadian home years later.

My two young unmarried aunts and uncle lived at my grandmother's house, occupying odd-shaped bedrooms, and three of my aunts who lived in nearby towns also came to visit us. All the names of the aunts began with the prefix "Dil," which means "heart." I had memorized these names by chanting them out loud, although I was soon to discover that each aunt had a nickname as well. The pet names, bestowed by my grandmother, were both comical and intimate.

My two young aunts were in their early twenties. The older one, Dil-Nashin, was studying at university. She smoked cigarettes secretly and tied her long braids in elaborate satin ribbons. There was a slender intensity to her and a regality to her posture. The younger one, Dilara, had saucer-sized eyes and a more robust frame. She had chosen to be a trainer for the Girl Guides Association and was brisk and athletic. Unknown to my grandmother, she took me on a secret visit to the rooftop terrace, where we children were forbidden to go. Here she informed me with mind-boggling nonchalance that one could slide down to the courtyard on a good strong rope using the appropriate knots.

I was fascinated by my youthful aunts, who were more like fun-filled older sisters, and spent hours at their dressing tables fiddling with the porcelain bowls of face powder topped with soft puffs, or browsing through the contents of their glass-fronted book cabinets. Yet it was the lure of my grandmother's kitchen that won me over. In this long room, almost studio lit by the glow of cooking fires, my grandmother sat on a woven rush stool and cooked. Close at hand was her assistant, who chopped, sliced and ground spices in a large black stone pestle, handing them to her at intervals.

My grandmother's examination of the platters of sliced meats and vegetables was deliberate and intense. When I visited the kitchen, my grandmother would invite me to sit on a similar stool across from her. She treated me as a favoured guest and fed me morsels of food in various stages of being cooked, with a warning not to drop anything on my pretty dress.

My uncle Zahir, a tall, good-looking man with a shock of wavy auburn hair, also showed me favouritism, singling me out from my siblings and talking to me as though I were his peer. He wore long mufflers over wool jackets and had exquisite manners. Some of his long absences from the house were reported to be visits to the local cinema. He was a voracious reader, and books, magazines and newspapers surrounded his bed in an overwhelming profusion. Talking about my uncle's bedroom, which no one was allowed to tidy up, was the only time I heard a weary, defeated ring to my grandmother's voice. He worked for a radio station composing a political program, called *Voice of Kashmir,* which beamed out messages of solidarity from the Kashmiris in Pakistan to those who had opted to stay in India.

One day my uncle mesmerized me with a lecture on the perfect ankles of American film star Marilyn Monroe and the works of British author D.H. Lawrence. Just as he was saying that in a few years I should read Lawrence to discover the mysteries of love, I was alerted to activity in the courtyard below. Distracted, I excused myself and raced downstairs.

In the courtyard sat a tall man with my grandmother, who was pulling strange-looking beige tubes from a straw basket. She placed them with great reverence on a metal platter. The final item she took from the basket was a bouquet of tiny green leaves. I saw her hold them close to her face and inhale deeply. This was fenugreek, a herb used to flavour both meat and vegetable dishes with a pungent, lingering fragrance.

My grandmother motioned to me to come forward and informed me that lotus root with fenugreek herb would be cooked for lunch. Had I ever seen a lotus flower? When I shook my head I saw a shadow flit across her face. In this new heaven, she said, referring to the new homeland of Pakistan, we have to look in special places to find ourselves. She told me that lotus grew in Dal Lake in Srinagar, Kashmir, within walking distance of Bashirabad. However, lotus also grew in ponds a hundred kilometres outside the city of Rawalpindi.

Like the mango, the lotus flower had inspired design. In ancient Hinduism, which predated Islam in India, the lotus was the first symbol of creation, denoting life floating on the surface of water. The liberal Mughal emperor Akbar's first act of assimilation was to choose a Hindu wife and pay reverence to the flower associated with her culture. Mughal paintings depicted the lotus, and it was a popular architectural motif. In the Taj Mahal, the palace Shah Jehan built to celebrate his love for his wife, a shaft of marble rises as a column with a lotus flower as its crown.

I had only seen photographs of the lotus flower. Its rarity and beauty glistened through the narrative my grandmother spun, yet the gift of the lotus roots had a greater meaning I was too young to understand.

Later, over lunch, I sat nervously eyeing the tureen of lotus shoots, as I grappled with the concept of eating something that grew underwater. My grandmother's eyes were fixed on me. It was not her habit to force anything on her grandchildren, yet I sensed an unspoken challenge. She seemed to be sending the message that within this dish was something more significant, and she wondered whether I would be able to detect it. I tried to visualize beautiful lotus flowers springing out of the dining table but found it difficult to go underwater to the roots. Despite the murmurs of appreciation around the dining table, I remain gripped by fear. If I disliked the first taste, how would I conceal it from my grandmother, whom I only wanted to please?

Finally, I reached out for the serving spoon and placed one spiral of lotus shoot with some sauce on the rice on my plate. As I chewed the first mouthful, two unique flavours burst on my palate. However, it would take me at least two decades to identify the perfect marriage of tastes. The light straw-like flavour of the soft fibre fused with the pungent herb. The airy consistency of the dish itself was delicious—the first mouthful was almost existential, in that it was everything and nothing at the same time.

In time I grew to love this dish, for I had witnessed how my grandmother's lost paradise visited her more often than she imagined. To my grandmother, the spirals of lotus roots swimming in the infused sauce were flavoured with nostalgia. In her hands, this was how the emotional component of cuisine revealed itself—by converting food into lived history.

Before the end of that visit, my grandmother served another memorable dish, which would forever make lunch a favourite meal for me. Even in my adult years, my grandmother's notion that the day must be punctuated mid-point by glorious food stayed with me. When I was first exposed to Spanish and Latin cultures, whose main meal of the day is lunch, followed by a long siesta, my thoughts flew to my grandmother.

The creation of one particular lunch dish and its accompanying drama became a high point in our family history. Tamatar paneer is a Kashmiri dish of slices of lightly fried cottage cheese, resembling a firmer version of buffalo mozzarella, atop a sauce of spiced fresh tomatoes. The finest-quality cheese came only from the city of Peshawar in the North-West Frontier province of Pakistan, where it was sold early in the mornings. My grandmother announced that someone who was travelling on a plane would deliver the cheese to her house. This was a rare occasion, as air travel at the time was considered an act of daring extravagance. True to her Mughal heritage, my grandmother viewed this venture with the same equanimity as her ancestors, who transported cooling melons by elephant to the searing plains of India. Her anxiety surfaced only when she mused about the freshness of the cheese and its time of arrival. A sense of excitement infused the playful atmosphere of H196 Murree Road, as we all wondered in the last remaining days of the trip if the cheese would arrive in time.

When it arrived the day before we were to leave, our excitement had reached such proportions it was as though fireworks had exploded in the central courtyard of the house. A large green Thermos opened to reveal a round of cheese wrapped in shiny green leaves, secured by a white cotton string. With a paring knife, my grand-mother cut a small slice and chewed it thoughtfully for a few seconds. No one was offered a sample. She then disappeared into the kitchen.

When I crept in an hour later, a magical sight greeted me, one that remains part of the ambience of this dish, on the rare occasions when I make it. A crimson stew of fresh tomatoes and herbs bubbled in a large pan, and my grandmother's alabaster face was tinted with a delicate flush, transforming her into a medieval sorceress melting precious rubies. Later, when she placed the rectangles of golden fried cheese on the surface of the tomatoes and added a garnish of finely chopped cilantro, I was not offered a sample. Instead, the first seeds of the delights of anticipation were implanted in my mind. At lunch, with the accompaniment of steamed basmati rice, each delicious morsel burst with a tang of fresh tomatoes stewed to perfection with garlic and black cumin and complemented by the creamy acidity of the cheese.

꧁

Recently, I witnessed a similar ritual in the home of a friend in Toronto. My friend convulsed with anticipatory delight at the expected arrival of fresh Atlantic lobster, which her son was bringing on a two-hour flight from Halifax. He would get home by lunchtime, she informed me. The attention to the quality of the food and the excitement at its transportation were identical. It was reassuring to note that Mughals were alive and well in all parts of the world.

This lunch also made me nostalgic for my mother's Friday lunches. She served fish and seafood on Fridays, as this was the day when meat was not sold in the markets of Karachi. There was no religious reason for the prohibition—it was simply a bureaucratic injunction issued by the government. Although my mother had a fully staffed household, she purchased the fish herself. Detecting freshness and ensuring that fish was filleted precisely was a lesson she had learned from her mother, my beloved grandmother.

Lotus Shoots and Fenugreek *(Nadru)*

Lotus shoots are available in Chinese fresh produce markets. Garam masala is a spice mixture of cardamom, cinnamon, cumin, black pepper and bay leaves. It can be purchased premixed, both ground and unground, at any Indian or Pakistani grocery store. To grind fresh garam masala, empty the contents of one premixed package into a spice or coffee grinder and grind to the consistency of finely ground coffee.

2 pounds fresh lotus shoots
2 tablespoons vegetable oil
1-inch piece fresh ginger, ground to a paste
4 whole cloves
2 teaspoons coriander powder
1 teaspoon black cumin seeds
1/2 teaspoon garam masala
2 green chilies
Salt to taste
1 large bunch fresh fenugreek leaves
1 cup water

Cut the lotus shoots diagonally into thin slices and wash well, cleaning out any soil from the cavities. Heat the oil in a large, heavy skillet over medium heat and fry the lotus shoots until golden brown. Remove and set aside. Add the remaining spices to the pan and fry, stirring often, for about 2 minutes. Lower the heat and place the lotus shoots on the fried paste. Cover with the fenugreek leaves and pour in the water. Cover the pan and simmer for 15 minutes, or until the lotus is soft. Serve spooned over steamed rice.

Serves 6.

3

Okra Transformed by Crushed Pomegranate Seeds

LOOK TO THE BLOWING ROSE ABOUT US—"LO,
LAUGHING," SHE SAYS, "INTO THE WORLD I BLOW:
AT ONCE THE SILKEN TASSEL OF MY PURSE
TEAR, AND ITS TREASURE ON THE GARDEN THROW."
—Omar Khayyam, *The Rubaiyat*

❧

My childhood home in Karachi was a sprawling one-storey structure surrounded by a stone wall. Following the width of the house in front was a stretch of lawn bordered by a prickly hedge. A gateway led to a gravel driveway, at the end of which was the garage, its green door fastened with a padlock. A large backyard was filled with wild almond trees, a small open water tank and a enormous vegetable garden.

The house was on a quiet residential street where government officials resided. My mother, Dilafroze, ran this household like an army general, conducting inspections and spot checks, and even managing my debonair father, with his penchant for reciting couplets of verse over the dining table. If my grandmother was like a ship of state, my mother was a pirate ship, with a skull-and-bones flag rippling over chests of treasure.

It was in her nature to uproot mediocrity of any kind. She presided over a domestic staff of five and trained the cooks impeccably—they bore the stamp of being "Dilafroze trained." There was also a cyclonic speed to her own activities. If unexpected guests arrived, refreshments were served immediately.

She was a celebrated cook, whose recipes were requested by the endless stream of guests and relatives at the dining table. I often loitered in the big dining room before these dinner parties, watching the staff arrange the napkins and flatware on the immaculate linen. The gardener would bring in tight clusters of flowers and place them in silver glasses on the table. I could never muster the courage to tell my mother that the bouquets should be released, even strewn around the dinner plates. From my vantage, the entire universe adored my spellbinding mother, and it would have been an act of unimaginable folly to challenge such perfection.

⚜

My mother was born in Srinagar, Kashmir, and spent her adolescence at Bashirabad, her parents' home. She was the eldest of eight siblings, who deferred to her judgment throughout her life and adored her as the family favourite. When she was born, the word *mubarik,* which means "congratulations," was heard so frequently that this became her pet name. Academically gifted, she wanted to study medicine, but her autocratic father informed her that it would be difficult to combine married life with a demanding profession. She was sent instead to the college for women, affiliated with Punjab University, in the city of Lahore, where she studied English literature and graduated as a gold medallist.

A beautiful and high-spirited young woman, my mother caught my father's eye at the Srinagar train station on her way home for the summer vacation. My father, Anwar, had accompanied her eldest stepbrother, Bashir, to collect her at the station in a small horse-drawn carriage, called a *tonga.* The next day my thoroughly infatuated father came for a visit on the pretext of seeing her brother, in hopes of catching another glimpse of the young woman who had dazzled him. She was nowhere in sight, but lying in the sitting room was a copy of *Hamlet* with her name written on it, which he promptly stole. To the love-smitten man, even a book touched by her hands was precious. My mother futilely engaged in full-scale sibling warfare over the missing book, only to discover after her marriage that my father was the culprit.

My parents' wedding took place in the family home, Bashirabad. As her life shifted from university student to young wife and mother, she continually expanded her cooking repertoire, embracing trends and different cuisines. After spending a year obtaining her graduate degree in the United States, she went on a shopping rampage, shipping ovens, electrical mixers and other modern appliances home to Pakistan to improve her kitchen.

❦

The kitchen of our Karachi home was located off the dining room. Unlike my grandmother, my mother never encouraged me to enter her kitchen. It was as though my mother were a brilliant scientist performing important work in her laboratory, and my status as a child did not permit me to understand the mysteries of her kitchen.

In this combat zone, coal-burning stoves hissed and shot out sparks. Cords attached to electric stoves with ringed burners regularly shorted out and blew out the wall switches. On shelves, black stone pestles and mortars were lined up like implements of war rather than cuisine. Cast-iron plates called *tawas* were heated on the stove to cook chapatis, rounds of delicate whole-wheat flour bread that puffed up with air. Long after being removed from the stove, the plates retained their heat and had to be held with a wad of cloth to avoid singed fingers. Water flowed endlessly from a large brass faucet above a trough-style sink, next to which sat a bottle of potassium permanganate solution, a lurid fuchsia liquid that we called "pinky," used to wash vegetables. A hissing pressure cooker with a stopper-covered valve bobbed on the stove, carrying the threat of explosions that could send scalding food up to the heavens. Large pots of boiling water for washing dishes filled the room with steam.

Amid this chaos, two male cooks whirled like acrobats to prepare the meals my mother planned daily. When she appeared in the kitchen to taste and give directions or to prepare something herself, a reverential hush fell over the room.

A screen door led off the kitchen to the back garden, and another door led to the storeroom. Here, dry provisions such as flour, sugar, tins of vegetable oil, vats of ghee (clarified butter), bottles of vinegar, home-made preserves and large sacks of rice were stored. Many years later I discovered that in most Pakistani homes the storeroom was locked to prevent the staff from pilfering, yet in my mother's home it was always unlocked, for she had ultimate trust in the people she employed.

Although I wasn't allowed in the kitchen, I spent many hours in the pantry. A large American refrigerator hummed in this room. There were cupboards and shelves crammed with crockery, food containers and large wide-mouthed Thermoses lined with silvery glass. Against one wall was a large counter where prepared food was brought in from the kitchen and arranged on platters.

To me, the pantry was an endless source of fascination and something of a divining rod. If a random visit revealed that dessert bowls were lined up, I knew that guests were coming for dinner. A scattering of bread crumbs suggested that sandwiches would appear for tea. Cut-glass bowls filled with mint chutney meant that chickpea flour fritters were about to be served. I would race back and share this news with my incorrigible brother, Shahid, who once hollowed out a dessert so that when it was cut the entire form collapsed before my mother's eyes.

My brother and I often teamed up to commit hugely successful crimes in the pantry. Although he was a year older than me, I was a perfect accomplice, for I could run faster than him and would not dissolve into a puddle of tears if I scraped a knee. One daring midnight raid on the pantry took place just before the feast that would end the thirty-day fast of Ramadan. The night before the feast, after the new moon was sighted, my mother prepared many desserts herself. Chopped nuts and silver foil decorated the desserts, laid out on the long pantry shelves or placed in the refrigerator to chill overnight. The quantity was overwhelming, as we expected many guests on the feast day.

After most of the household was asleep, my brother and I, clad in pyjamas, rendezvoused outside his bedroom, located some distance from mine. We picked our way on bare feet through the dark house and headed for the pantry, where we lifted a bowl or two of dessert and dashed back to his room. Sitting on his bed, we stuffed ourselves with puddings drenched with the scent of roses and cardamom, each spoonful tasting better than it ever had because of our clandestine caper. As children, we were creating our own ambience for eating the desserts, and we had yet to master the delights of anticipation.

My mother had a uniquely developed social conscience, and feast day would not begin for us until the needy were given food as well. On prominent feast days, she took hampers to the local mosques, where she distributed the food with her own hands. Each parcel of food was wrapped in kite paper and tied with coloured string. Kite paper had a thin rustling texture and the weight of tissue and came in vibrant greens, blues and reds. In the heat the colour would bleed from the paper and stain both the food and my mother's hands, yet with her thoroughly Mughal temperament, she prized aesthetics over organic-dye ingestion.

❧

My mother viewed social injustice as a personal challenge, and so it was no surprise that her political conscience was equally well developed. My parents had been actively involved in the nationalist politics that led to the founding of Pakistan in 1947. When my father was imprisoned for his loyalty to Mohammad Ali Jinnah, the founder of Pakistan, my mother held the fort in Srinagar, taking care of her toddlers while somehow finding the time to perfect her carrot and almond preserve. This preserve, regarded as having medicinal properties that boosted the immune system, consisted of chunks of carrots and large white unsliced almonds in a golden fluid that tasted like perfumed spring flowers. My mother sent jars to the prison where my father was held in solitary confinement for three months. Of course, a cube of sugar once a week was the only allocation that ever came his way. Had he known that his jailors were consuming the carrot preserve, he would have tunnelled his way out of his concrete cell and fought for it as well.

My siblings and I would race to the dining table each night to consume these morsels of our parents' exciting political history along with the mouth-watering meals. We were citizens of the new country of Pakistan. Yet losing an ancestral homeland was no excuse for coming home without perfect report cards or displaying bad table manners. Over dinner, my father also recounted the story of my mother embroidering late at night the flags of the new nation of Pakistan, which were handed out secretly in the markets of Indian-occupied Kashmir. It was as though the platters of food on the large dining table were flavoured with another set of dazzling ingredients.

Pride, acts of heroism, searing loss and blinding victory coiled through the fragrant steam rising from dishes.

I admired my dramatic mother and regarded her as a font of love, humour, passion and artistry. She was a magnificent cook who raised the standards of cuisine to such a level that I was hesitant for years to experiment myself. Although she never taught me how to cook, I was sensitized to discern flavours and techniques simply by listening to her. She was the most confident person I knew. As far as she was concerned there were no shortcuts to good cooking, and every crisis in the kitchen could be redeemed.

One year, she decided to duplicate Heinz tomato ketchup. Rows of tomatoes were planted in the large vegetable garden. Trucks drove up carrying fresh manure. My father took his morning walks around the vegetable garden to check on the progress of the plants. Finally, when the tomatoes ripened and were picked, the infamous ketchup-making operation began. For two days, the dining room, kitchen and pantry became a food factory. Bottles were sterilized, filled with a red liquid and capped, and each batch was labelled. What appeared at the dining table bore very little resemblance to the American ketchup my siblings and I preferred, but no one could muster the courage to inform my mother.

Years later, she confessed that the entire project had been a disaster, and promptly added that she knew exactly where her error lay. I buried her secret and chuckled about it, thinking how valiantly my father had conspired with me and my siblings.

My memories of my mother are also tinged with tender maternal touches. Although as a toddler I could be fed anything, by age nine I had become a finicky eater and disliked organ meats of any kind. If sweetbreads or kidneys, great favourites of my father, were cooked, there would be two lamb cutlets resting on my plate.

She had an intimate knowledge of all of her children's tastes and dislikes. If we fell sick she would sit bedside and feed us with her own hands. The mother love flowing from her fingertips made each morsel of rice steamed in milk and sugar taste like the rarest delicacy. It was almost worth feigning illness simply to have her feed me. The sensorial delight of sucking on her fingertips may well have sensitized me at an early age to acts of tenderness that lead in adulthood to erotic play. In this act of maternal intimacy, she followed the traditions of her Mughal ancestors, who cooked, served and ate with their hands. My mother, educated both in the East and the West, forbade her children to use their fingers at the table yet chose on occasion to dispense with her own mandate.

My mother had an uncanny ability to gauge my thoughts, and it was easy for her to discern which child had disobeyed her. Most school mornings found me in the dining room at war with my breakfast. The hated boiled egg and the tall glass of warm buffalo milk coated with heavy cream confronted me with nauseating regularity. I would lean out the window and throw the egg and milk into the jungle of zinnia flowers below, then eat with relish the buttered toast with honey and leave for school.

While on his morning walks, my father often noticed eggshells glistening in the bushes but simply buried them deeper in the foliage. However, one day my mother accompanied him on his walk. The next morning I was summoned to her bedroom. Next to her bed was a little table, and resting on it was my breakfast of the boiled egg accompanied by the glass of milk and toast. My mother told me that the choice was simple: either I consumed the entire breakfast or I stayed home from school. I was also given a textbook lecture on starving children and my unconscionable attitude. Although I would have much preferred her rose-scented, pistachio-studded rice flour pudding, I obediently swallowed the boiled egg with gulps of milk. It was a preordained victory for my mother and a lesson to me that food must be appropriate for the occasion.

❦

Food and drink featured in most Mughal illustrated manuscripts of the fifteenth century. In the 1590s, royal artisans presented the Mughal emperor Akbar with an illustrated manuscript called the *Chingiznama*, which contained more than 190 illustrations and was first translated from the Turki script to the revised Persian script. In one of the most politically significant illustrations, the Mongol leader Chingiz Khan was shown dividing his empire between his sons. Platters of food and drink surrounded the imperial central dais, and at the bottom of the miniature painting, a line of attendants carried food on covered platters. Despite the daunting circumstances of the event, the presence of food and drink civilized the gathering.

To my mother, creating ambience to complement a meal was equally important, and her picnics can only be described as courtly. In the daisy-strewn hillsides of northern Pakistan, where we had a summer home, we would set forth in a small procession, accompanied by our aging nursemaid and at least one domestic staff member. Rolled carpets, gramophones with records of Indian love songs, charcoal braziers, enamelled tin plates, wicker baskets and Thermos flasks were carried with us. Sometimes badminton racquets and a tenniquot rubber ring, which my brother used more as an assault weapon than a simple catch-and-throw device, were brought along.

What my mother orchestrated was to delight us in all ways possible. It was in her picnics that she displayed her passion for creating mood. The formality of the dining table was abandoned, as we lolled about on cushions and old fading carpets surrounded by fields and wildflowers. Food choices and portions were no longer mandatory. Even my mother became a bit of a gypsy, her silken clothes fluttering in the breeze and strands of hair escaping from her sleek chignon. Witnessing her transformation was a delight that was further enhanced by the food.

On one picnic, when I was about ten years old, she cooked an intricate dish on a charcoal brazier: layered *parathas*, flatbread stuffed with ground beef, onions, tomatoes, green chilies and coriander seeds, fried in pure ghee on a flat iron tawa. The pastry had been kneaded at home and moulded into small balls. Sitting on the grass, my mother rolled out perfect discs with a rolling pin on a wooden board. Her helper fanned the charcoal in the brazier so the embers glowed steadily. I watched with awe as my mother sprinkled the ground-beef mixture on the near-transparent pastry circles and covered them with another layer without breaking the delicate paratha. The filling retained its moisture as it cooked between the layers of pastry, which turned a golden bisque, and a cucumber and yogourt raita sauce accompanied the dish.

The tour de force of this picnic was the horseradish paratha, which I had always resisted because I did not care for the sting of horseradish. My mother, who believed that everything should be sampled once, won me over by creating a miniature paratha with my initials scored deeply into the top layer. It was mine, she pointed out, and no one else was allowed to eat it. The flavoured exclusivity, or so I thought, appealed to my fledgling vanity and I ate the paratha. It has remained a favourite of mine. Food is also an adventure, was the message my mother imparted, and presentation can be appealing and seductive. Two decades later, I replayed this scene in my Canadian kitchen by scoring the initials of my own daughters into miniature parathas.

❦

In my parents' home, a typical meal comprised a meat, fish or fowl entree accompanied by at least two vegetables, a yogourt salad and chutney. My parents were partial to exotic vegetables, and odd-shaped root vegetables, bitter gourds and string beans of unusual colour appeared periodically at the table. My parents' enthusiastic response was mystifying. They narrated the history of the vegetable and hailed its seasonal appearance as a near miracle. A typical child, I shied away from vegetables with unusual consistencies or tastes. However, the rule at the dining table was that everything had to be tasted before articulating preference or dislike.

One vegetable I disliked was okra, a vegetable laden with seeds and with a fine, gelatinous inner membrane. Although cooking partially dissolves the sticky interior, I made it a point to avoid it until the day my mother

transformed okra by stuffing it with crushed pomegranate seeds.

The pomegranate tree grows in central Asia, Persia and
northern India. In Hindu mythology, it is thought to
have been the tree of knowledge. In Greek mythology, the
goddess Demeter lost her daughter Persephone to Hades,
the god of the underworld, because she ate one grain
of the pomegranate fruit.

In Mughal paintings, men and women are shown
holding the beautiful red flowers of the pomegranate
tree. A famous courtesan who fell in love with the
Mughal emperor Akbar's son was called Anarkali, which
means "pomegranate blossom." The emperor had the
courtesan buried alive in a wall of bricks to prevent his
son from marrying her. In the city of Lahore, where
much Mughal architecture still stands, an entire market-
place is called Anarkali. The market is known for glass
bangles, embroidered silks and shoes decorated with
gold thread.

Persian cuisine flourished under emperors Darius
and Cyrus, dazzling both Alexander the Great and the
Mughals with its flavours enhanced by dried pomegranate seeds instead of lemons. The fruit itself is a large
crimson globe encased in tough leathery skin, with ruby
seeds inside encased in a white membrane. Removing
the membrane is time consuming and arduous; however,
the seeds are filled with delicious sweet-and-sour juice.

The juice is drunk on its own or added to sherbets, and the seeds are dried and crushed to a fine paste.

The day my mother served okra remains etched in my mind. She had slit the okra down the centre and removed the seeds and viscous membrane, then stuffed the pods with pomegranate seed paste and browned them over sautéed onions and spices. That day at lunch, my father took his first taste and closed his eyes for a moment. He appeared to be in a trance. Then he opened his eyes and simply gazed at my mother. She gave him a mischievous nod, and something flashed in her eyes that led me to believe she had prepared the dish solely for his pleasure. At that moment my parents were transformed. They were no longer just my benevolent custodians—they were also romantic lovers. Looking back, I realize that I had witnessed the enactment of love, and the instrument of pleasure was food.

My mother often surprised me with these tantalizing glimpses of her womanhood. At these moments she became the beautiful, high-spirited young woman my father had fallen in love with. My love for the pomegranate fruit in all its forms is based on the awareness that romantic love existed not only in fairy tales, but also in my parents.

Okra Stuffed with Pomegranate Seeds
(Anardana Bhari Bhindi)

This vegetable dish can be cooled and served as an appetizer. Served hot, it is a delicate accompaniment to both grilled and stewed meats. It also can be served on its own with either rice or whole-wheat flour chapatis; the starch absorbs the tartness of the pomegranate. During the steaming process, a small amount of the stuffing may ooze out. Allow it to spread naturally over the sides of the pod. Okra is a seasonal vegetable and can be purchased at South Asian and Caribbean stores. It is also widely used in the Creole cuisine of the southern United States. Dried pomegranate seeds can be purchased in South Asian and Middle Eastern grocery stores.

1 1/2 pounds fresh okra
2 bunches fresh coriander, leaves plucked
2 green chilies
4 tablespoons plus 1/4 cup water
1 cup dried pomegranate seeds
4–5 tablespoons vegetable oil
2 large onions, thinly sliced
3 cloves garlic, ground to a paste
1-inch piece fresh ginger, ground to a paste
1/2 teaspoon cayenne
1/2 teaspoon aniseed
Salt to taste

Trim and clean the okra. Using a sharp knife, make a small slit in the centre of the pod. With a demitasse or marrow spoon, dislodge and spoon out the seeds. If a pod breaks in the process, discard it, as the stuffing will ooze out.

To prepare the stuffing, place the coriander, chilies and 4 tablespoons of the water in a food processor; process for a few seconds until well mixed. Grind the pomegranate seeds to a paste in a spice or coffee grinder. Stir into the coriander mixture. Stuff the okra and set aside.

Heat the oil in a large, shallow skillet over medium heat and fry the onions until dark brown and caramelized. Remove with a slotted spoon and set aside. Add the garlic, ginger, cayenne, aniseed and salt to the pan and sauté over medium heat for 2 minutes. Blend in the remaining 1/4 cup water with a spoon. Turn the heat to low and gently place the okra over the fried spice mixture. Cover the pan and allow the okra to steam until tender, about 10 minutes. Sprinkle with the caramelized onions and serve immediately.

Serves 6.

4

My Mother's Legendary Biryani

And when Thyself with shining Foot shall pass
Among the Guests Star-scattered on the Grass,
And in thy joyous Errand reach the Spot
Where I made one—turn down an empty Glass!
—Omar Khayyam, *The Rubaiyat*

❧

Amid one glorious summer vacation in the northern hills of Pakistan, my mother slipped in an hour of math exercises each day so I could improve my scholastic record. I was fifteen and would sit for the International Baccalaureate exam within six months. My score on the end-of-term math exam had been dismal and was accompanied by that notorious comment, "she does not apply herself." The censure of Sister Longina Maria, principal of St. Joseph's Convent School, had invaded my summer Eden. My mother picked up the gauntlet with steely resolve and informed me that I had the entire summer to remedy this patently mistaken notion.

While the rest of my siblings galloped on horses through mountain forests, I was confined each morning to my bedroom. A small dish of almonds sat on my desk, placed there by my mother, who informed me that almonds were food for the brain. I chewed one almond after another, but the large boulder of fear that blocked my brain did not move. Outside, the world exploded with beauty as the mountain winds rustled the leaves of walnut trees and the sun blazed through a pure blue sky.

Our summer home was in a small town called Abbottabad, nestled in a valley ringed by mountains. This was the gateway to the soaring mountain ranges, glaciers and lakes of the north, bordering the frontiers of China, Afghanistan and Russia. In this region, called Hazara, the people bore the Mughal stamp in their chiselled features and flat Mongolian faces. Their eyes and hair were light coloured, and their fair complexions were reddened by the mountain sun. Their clothing, made of homespun wool called *patu,* gave them a ceremonial air. Although the men wore the standard Pakistani outfit of a long tunic over ballooning trousers, they also donned waistcoats, caps and shawls. As a child, I felt they were from a different world.

North of the little town of Abbottabad, roads spiralled upward to mountains and the breathtaking splendour of the Kaghan Valley, where rivers pounded through boulder-laden courses and offered fish and game. Some of the townspeople had come from the little mountain kingdoms of Swat, Hunza and Gilgit to the more temperate climate of Abbottabad. In this collection of versatile people, many sought employment in our home as cooks.

Our summer home was a rustic wooden structure with high ceilings, draughty rooms, slate tile floors and a garden filled with fruit trees. The plumbing was temperamental, and an array of local workmen would appear at all hours to correct the faucets and check the bathroom drains. Water was heated by immersing an electrical wand into a bucket of water and waiting for ten minutes for the water to warm up. Not blessed with patience, I often had icy-cold showers so I could dress before my sister, Mahjabin, whose length of stay in the bathroom could rival a Mughal courtesan's languorous toilette.

The kitchen was cavernous and rustic. Local clay and copper pots were used for cooking, and vegetables were stored in straw baskets. In one corner of the room sat the *hamam,* a brass pot-bellied contraption about a metre high that supplied hot water. Like the samovar, the hamam contained a chamber in which heated coals and wood were inserted and lit. Two spigots in the front released the boiling water. The hamam was kept lit all morning and then in the evenings, for despite the rustic environment, my mother refused to part with the accoutrements she was partial to.

Each summer a set of maternal aunts, uncles and their children visited. The sweeping front veranda of this home was the site for chess matches between my father and my aunts' husbands. He viewed his chess victories as an appropriate ego-deflating device for his opponents. Some of these matches lasted all day, with breaks for food and tea. Homemade lemonade and fruit sherbets were served in thick bottle-glass tumblers, set out on hand-loomed cotton tablecloths with bright designs. The serving dishes, dinner plates and cups and saucers, ordered by my mother from the Gujrat pottery factory, were twice the size of those at home. She felt that the bracing mountain air resulted in heartier appetites, and the quantities of both guests and food could be better served in this outlandish dishware.

Sometimes my father asked my mother if she planned to make her biryani for these family gatherings, but she always refused, saying that it was a dish meant to be made in peace. She also believed that the children of the house were too young to appreciate it, which raised its mystique in my eyes. Despite our collective wishes, she never did make biryani in our mountain home.

My father joined us for only a few weeks each summer, because his vacation from work was not as long as our school holidays. His arrival was marked with great excitement. An impassioned history buff, he related historical anecdotes as we drove through the mountains or rambled through the countryside. He also managed to disrupt my mother's regimens and carefully planned menus.

Some mornings, my father took a jaunt to the inner bazaar of the town simply to talk to local shopkeepers and roadside vendors. He would return with sweets my mother frowned upon or scratchy wool caps that never fit anyone in the family. Another favourite indulgence was having the village barber come to the house and shave him seated outside in the garden. I would observe this ritual in terror, for to me the fierce-looking man looming over my father's lathered face had the appearance of a brigand. However, my father also knew that when fresh trout caught in the Kaghan Valley arrived, the barber doubled as fishmonger. Trout fried in white unsalted butter procured from the military dairy in town was a dish only my mother prepared. It was the singular treat of the summer, arriving unexpectedly even in the dead of night, as the winding roads from the valley were difficult to traverse with speed.

My mother was also the last to know when he issued one of his regular invitations to half the nation to visit him in his country home. On one occasion, the nation's head of state, who was a friend of my father's, dropped in, bringing a convoy of security officers, with crackling handheld radios, who surrounded the house. A terrified servant burst into the living room to announce that soldiers had come to arrest the entire household.

My mother made no distinction between the tea served to the president outside in the garden or to the security officers ringed outside the gate. Savoury pastries and sizzling chickpea flour fritters stuffed with onions and potatoes were churned out at great speed. Gallons of tea brewed in kettles and then transferred into teapots were arranged on trays with pitchers of warm milk and sent out. Kashmiri hospitality knew no limits, and my mother fiercely embraced this mantra of etiquette.

My father did not cook, repair gadgets or even understand the workings of the cars he drove on occasion. Instead, he was an excellent bridge player, powerful swimmer and skilled chess player, who also recited poetry spontaneously and loved adventure. He had chosen our summer mountain home as compensation for the property he had lost in Srinagar, for he believed his family needed the contrasting charm of the country to balance out life in the cosmopolitan capital city of Karachi.

In the same way, although he appreciated the varied delights offered at his table, he was drawn to organic food as a means of embracing a more holistic lifestyle. During some of our country drives, we children prayed fervently that a flock of goats would not appear by the side of the road. This always meant that my father would stop the car and request a cup of fresh goat's milk, which we were then to sample because it was excellent for the health. The sour taste and the high odour invariably induced a ripple of nausea, and we would back off in terror, only to be accused of being weak kneed.

One summer, my father planned a special trip. We would leave our beloved mountains for the town of Sialkot, near the Indian border in eastern Punjab, to visit the seat of his paternal ancestors who had owned a paper mill in the region. He wanted to make a charitable donation to honour his ancestors, and we were to meet some distant relatives who still lived there. It was a family trip, and my father would drive us himself.

The next morning, he sat jauntily behind the wheel of a mid-sized German car, ignoring the worried look of the family driver. Next to him sat my mother, knitting a sea-green wool sweater, and the children piled into the back seat. It would be a four-hour drive.

By mid-morning, the lamb and mint chutney sandwiches packed for the trip had been demolished. We looked out of the moving car at the roadside food stalls. However, my mother had banned both the streetside *pakora,* a deep-fried fritter, and jugs of maroon pomegranate juice. The words *germs* and *a good way to get hepatitis* made tempers rise along with appetites in the back seat.

My father placated us by promising that a real treat lay ahead. We would have lunch at the famous Amelia Hotel in the town of Sialkot. We were not used to dining out, with the rare exception of two Chinese restaurants in Karachi. There was also the spanking new Shezan restaurant, which served a tutti-frutti ice cream that made us feel as though we were living in the United States and jiving to Elvis Presley records. Many years later, I realized that the powdered milk ice cream topped with canned fruit cocktail paled in comparison to my mother's superb pistachio ice cream.

A hushed altercation seemed to be taking place in the front seat of the car. My mother, to our dismay, made a disparaging comment about taking children to the Amelia Hotel, at which point my father chuckled and said he wanted his children to taste the famous cuisine. Apparently, the hotel had a scandalous reputation of sorts, as the Anglo-Indian proprietor, Amelia, had serviced the local gentry in some unacceptable ways. Whether she mingled freely with her patrons or supplied sexual favours was never clearly established from the snatches of coded conversation lost in the mayhem of the back seat. However, when we reached the hotel and a lady with jangling gold bracelets and flaming red hair appeared to greet us, we tumbled out of the car with lightning speed.

We were ushered indoors to a large room sprinkled with rough wooden tables and chairs, the shabby blue velvet curtains in the entrance snapping shut behind us. My father announced that lunch of a single entree

accompanied by simple tandoori rotis was legendary at
the hotel. He smiled at my mother, who gave him a
mischievous smile.

The only item on the bare wooden table was cutlery
that had seen better days. A large metal jug of drinking
water and six equally crude metal tumblers were plonked
in the middle of the table. The first dish to arrive was a
salad composed of red radishes, tomatoes and red onion
rings, surrounded by fresh red chilies. It sat in a large
white enamelled plate looking like a garish oil painting. I had never seen a salad without a hint of green in
it. Yet the salad created a mood of its own on the table,
one that was positively rowdy. Within minutes, large
serving plates filled with food were set in front of us
with little ceremony. A braided straw basket of rotis,
bearing the crisp brown marking of the clay oven they had
been baked in, accompanied the food.

Although the meal appeared to be a simple chicken
curry, the first mouthful scooped up with a piece of roti
set waste to this notion. The exploding flavours ignited
a brushfire that travelled from the mouth to the brain and
then settled in the stomach. As a teenager with little
knowledge of cooking, I had no way of detecting how
this chicken curry was different from the one my mother
made. Yet many years later, when I cooked in my own
home, I realized that the flesh of the chicken had a
muscularity to the fibre that only freshly slaughtered

fowl has. The burned, brick-coloured gravy had a coarse simplicity that meant ordinary spices, rather than saffron and cardamom, had been used. The assault of large quantities of ground cayenne made sweat pour off our faces, yet we licked our plates clean.

Piling into the car after lunch and waving to Amelia, who threw a ravishing smile at my father, we sped off on the last leg of the journey. After fifteen minutes my father halted the car as the road suddenly ended. Two canopied horse-drawn carriages waited at the edge of a sea of mustard fields. The tonga had a regular seat in front next to the driver and a sloping one at the back, meaning the person seated up front rode in comfort, while those in the back had to grip the side rails. Dividing the children, my parents sat in separate tongas. As we drove, my father told us that we would eat fresh rotis made from corn that grew in the fields belonging to our relatives.

After a bumpy thirty-minute ride, a low cluster of whitewashed homes suddenly appeared ahead. Two tall men dressed in white waited in front. When we got down from the tongas, the men greeted my father with great affection. They were tall fair men with high colouring and light brown eyes. These were our Kashmiri cousins twice removed, on my father's side. They embraced us and led us inside.

The wives, draped in shawls, greeted my mother with reverence. A great deal of fuss was made of my brother, as he would carry the family name. Years later, I too would carry my father's name, but I'm not certain this would have received the same attention. I remember thinking that my father, dressed in a tweed jacket, wool trousers and cravat, could not possibly be part of this family. Yet it was fascinating to see our parents move with ease in homes made of whitewashed mud with no indoor plumbing.

The meal we ate that evening came from the land around us. Fresh buttermilk churned in clay pots was served in tumblers of ornately embellished metal. Mustard greens, which had been cooked overnight to the consistency of velouté, were topped with a pat of fresh homemade butter and accompanied by the corn flour rotis. Thin green chilies were the only condiment. Having been fire-proofed by Amelia's cuisine, I ate an entire one without flinching. It was a simple meal, yet it was also unique. A powdered grain added to the mustard greens mellowed their acidity, and the homemade butter filled me with a lifelong passion for using sweet butter in my own cooking. At the end of the meal, a large wash-basin and jug of water were presented. We washed our hands with a coarse granular soap and rinsed them in water in which a few rose petals floated.

I froze in shock when our hosts led us to the rooms we would sleep in. Simple woven hemp and wood-framed beds sat on bare floors, and tiny windows looked out over the surrounding fields. Yet as overnight guests, we were expected to behave with all the courtesy our hosts had displayed.

Later that night, we watched a clear black night studded with brilliant stars. The air was perfumed by the herbal tang of fields surrounding the house. Both the country food and the rural ambience gave me a greater appreciation for my father's infrequently articulated preference for the delights of country living. Also, observing the confidence with which our hosts offered us the simplest of meals was a matchless exercise in entertaining with grace. Before we left, my father donated a sum of money to have a community hall built in the vicinity, which would give the rural population a place to hold marriages or gather for funerals.

≋

When the summer holidays ended and we returned to our Karachi home, my mother re-established the order of our lives. Her meals were governed by the seasons. However, the predictable order was regularly punctuated by requests from her friends for dishes she was skilled at preparing.

One morning, an official flag car belonging to a cabinet minister rolled into our driveway. What emerged from the car was not guests, but baskets of fresh spinach and legs of lamb. The minister was a good friend of my parents and was hosting his first official dinner party. My mother was very fond of him, and she had offered to cook for him Kashmiri spinach and lamb.

My mother did the unthinkable and set to work in her dressing gown. A few hours later, a shriek of agony issued from the kitchen. It came from my mother and could only mean that some heart-rending tragedy had occurred. Apparently, the puréed spinach, which is added to the meat, had not been rinsed the appointed seven times and there was some sand in the prepared dish. None of us ventured toward the kitchen.

An hour later, my mother emerged smiling serenely, and half an hour later the official car drove away with the dish. The next morning, the minister, laden with flowers, sat with my parents extolling the virtues of spinach and lamb. My mother never revealed the secret of how she had saved the dish. From this I learned culinary execution is a matter of will, and above all one must live up to one's reputation.

≫≪

In the kitchen, my mother was like the invisible conductor of a brilliant symphony, with ingredients, utensils and techniques as the musical instruments. I was simply a member of the audience who was privileged to hear the music. To master the skills of cooking, I had to be part detective and part adventurer. The one exception was

biryani, a Mughal rice dish that as a child I never did
watch my mother make.

I was introduced to this dish on a Friday that began
uneventfully in our Karachi home. On Fridays, the Sabbath
of Muslims, schools, shops and offices closed at noon, and
domestic staff were given time off. The government had
declared this a meatless day to encourage the consumption of fish. Lunch was followed by a long afternoon
nap. However, on this particular Friday afternoon, my
mother was not in her bedroom. I was told that she was
in the kitchen preparing a special dish and could not be
disturbed. From the sounds emerging from the kitchen,
I could tell that the cook was also with her.

My father and I sauntered by the kitchen, and he
stuck his head in for a moment. Standing behind him,
all I could see were cooking pans and bowls arranged
on a table while my mother rubbed strands of saffron
and dropped them into a bowl. She did not glance up.
On this meatless day, packages of frozen meat had
emerged from the freezer and were being thawed. I
retreated as I had been instructed, yet I would regret
that decision for many years.

The legendary Mughal biryani is reputed to have been
brought into northern India in the late fourteenth
century by the great Mongolian conqueror Timur-I-
Lang, also know as Tamerlane. The dish belonged to
the Persians; the word *birian* in Farsi means "fried."

When Mughal emperor Aurangzeb seized the kingdom of Golconda in 1687, this was the premier dish of the largest princely state of India. In the eighteenth century, the royal court at Golconda, in the city of Hyderabad, had a reputation for attending more to the refinement of cuisine than to affairs of state. It was not the lure of the fabled gem treasury of the Asafjahi dynasty that drew Arab, Persian, Afghan and Turkish visitors, but the twenty-six varieties of biryani.

The biryani constitutes an entire meal. The dish is centred around rice and changes flavour depending on which meats, fish, herbs and vegetables are added. As the biryani spread throughout India, it collected regional ingredients and even various methods of assembly. The paella of Spain, the risotto of Italy and the pilafs of Arab and Mediterranean cultures are all related to the biryani. However, the Mughal biryani reigns supreme because of the incomparable quality of its two key ingredients: aged basmati rice and saffron. Both are widely cultivated locally and exported throughout the world. The finest basmati rice comes from Pakistan and the best saffron from Kashmir. Folklore suggests that the test of a true biryani is to throw a cupful of the cooked dish on the floor and see whether every grain of rice is separate—this will reveal that the finest basmati rice has been used.

The chefs of Golconda were inspired by Mughal architecture in embellishing their cuisine, and the gem-crusted Taj Mahal became a blueprint for the biryani. Rubies, emeralds, sapphires, diamonds and natural pearls bezelled in the marble were symbolized by the nuts, crystalline sugared fruits in brilliant hues and edible silver foil decorating the cooked biryani.

My mother's biryani was based on a recipe that had floated down to her from her parents' home in Kashmir. She would make it once or twice a year on ceremonial occasions, and never entrusted it to the trained cooks in her kitchen.

My mother had a great love of saffron, which was harvested in the valleys of Kashmir where she grew up, and used it liberally in many of her dishes, without much concern for its cost. Saffron is one of the costliest spices in the world, for it takes 225 000 stigmas of the crocus flower to make up a pound. Considered an aphrodisiac because of its warming qualities, saffron was included in the trousseaus of Kashmiri brides. The spice also was used as an organic dye for food; hence, saffron is also the name of a colour. To call something *zafrani* in Urdu means that which is red and gold.

My mother's preference for layering the biryani herself, without an audience, was part of the mystique of the dish. It was only after I married and left Pakistan for Canada that I observed her layering the dish, on my visits home. The layering is a fascinating ritual to observe, for the technique requires delicacy of touch and expertise in salting and gauging temperatures. Cooked ingredients are mingled with semi-cooked ones and steamed together. The biryani pot is often sealed with a ribbon of moist kneaded dough, which bakes with the heat to become a seal.

On the days my mother made her biryani, my father tiptoed around the house with a tremulous smile, regarding the operation in the kitchen as a sacred ritual. He told us that he considered all biryanis to be suspect except my mother's, and he refused to eat it in other people's homes. Alarmingly, I now find myself with the same attitude when I serve my own biryani: I wonder if it is an act of disloyalty to eat a biryani that has not been cooked by my mother.

Over the years, I collected scraps of paper on which I listed my mother's ingredients and measurements. I loved biryani but was daunted by the thought of cooking it myself. However, I was also a child of my family and endowed with a reckless desire for culinary showmanship. Finally, I thought I was ready to cook a biryani for a lunch I was throwing for thirty friends. The exercise was disastrous. I oversalted the biryani, and although my mother was continents away, I had to draw on her legacy of resilience and save my reputation. Like my mother, I also buried the solution to my culinary misadventure deep in my heart.

Conversations with my mother about biryani always made me hesitant to heap excessive verbal laurels on her cooking skills, for she exhibited a confidence that was bereft of vanity. All she would acknowledge was the response to her cooking displayed by her guests' appetites. I confessed to her that in my Canadian kitchen, friends ringed around me while I layered a biryani, and I considered this an exciting part of a dinner party. Unlike her, I did not require peace to make the dish. I felt that observing the act of layering the raw ingredients with the cooked ones raised the delights of anticipation. She simply smiled at me and replied that my attitude reminded her of her brother Amir, whom she considered to be an exceptional cook.

Mughal Biryani

This recipe can easily be halved or doubled. Serve it as a complete meal, accompanied by a sauce of grated cucumber or cooked eggplant and yogourt. Meat dishes have their own distinct flavour and should not be served with a biryani. Presented on a serving platter, the biryani is an attractive medley of white-and-orange saffron-dotted rice and chunks of lamb. Decorate it with *varak*, edible silver foil, which can be purchased in South Asian grocery stores in 3- by 6-inch strips, pressed onto tissue paper. It is very important not to fall in love and immediately decide to cook a biryani, as this could result in oversalting.

1/2 cup plus 1 tablespoon vegetable oil
6 medium onions, thinly sliced

1 teaspoon cayenne
7 cloves garlic, ground to a paste
3-inch piece fresh ginger, ground to a paste
1 cup blanched slivered almonds
2 1/2 pound leg of lamb, cubed, with bone
2 1/2 teaspoons salt
2 cups water
4 cups yogourt
4 whole cloves
3 pods black cardamom, seeds removed
1 teaspoon caraway seeds
6 large green chilies, finely chopped
1 small bunch fresh coriander, leaves plucked
6 stems fresh mint, leaves plucked
juice of 2 large lemons
4 1/2 cups aged basmati rice
2-inch-long cinnamon stick
1 teaspoon saffron, crushed and soaked in 1 cup
   hot water
1 cup milk
Edible silver foil, for decorating

Heat 1/2 cup of the oil in a large, deep skillet over
medium-high heat and fry the onions until dark brown
and caramelized. Remove with a slotted spoon and set
aside. Add the cayenne, garlic, ginger and almonds to the
skillet and fry, stirring, for about 3 minutes. Add the
lamb with the bone and 1/2 teaspoon of the salt. Brown
over high heat, 3 to 5 minutes. Lower the heat and pour
in 2 cups water, cooking, uncovered, over medium heat
until the lamb is tender and most of the water has
evaporated, about 1 hour. Remove from heat, discard

the bone and stir in the yogourt, cloves, cardamom, caraway seeds, chilies, coriander, mint and lemon juice.

Place rice in a large, heavy pot, adding enough water to cover the rice by 3 inches. Stir in the remaining 2 teaspoons salt and the cinnamon stick. Cook over high heat until the rice is parboiled, tasting it to determine whether it has lost its granular hardness and is two-thirds cooked. Strain the rice in a large colander, discarding the cinnamon stick, and set aside.

Clean the pot and add the remaining tablespoon of vegetable oil, rotating the pot so the oil covers the bottom. Start layering the biryani by placing a layer of rice in the pot and sprinkling the lamb mixture on top. Then sprinkle a layer of caramelized onions over the lamb mixture. Using a small spoon, dot the surface with the saffron water. Repeat the layers until the ingredients are finished. Pour the milk over the last layer.

Cover the pot and make certain it is well sealed. If necessary, place another smaller heavy pot upside down over the cover. Cook over low heat about 10 to 15 minutes until the rice is completely cooked, checking after 10 minutes. The grains of rice should become soft.

Using a saucer, scoop up the biryani and arrange it on a large platter. Decorate it with edible silver foil by pressing strips onto the surface and lifting off the backing paper so the foil clings to the food.

Serves 8 to 10.

5

A Gift of
Wild Black Mushrooms
from Uncle Amir

IRAM INDEED IS GONE WITH ALL ITS ROSE,
AND JAMSHYD'S SEV'N-RING'D CUP WHERE NO ONE KNOWS;
BUT STILL THE VINE HER ANCIENT RUBY YIELDS,
AND STILL A GARDEN BY THE WATER BLOWS.
—Omar Khayyam, *The Rubaiyat*

❧

With my first glimpse of my uncle Amiruddin Dar, I
felt as though I were in the presence of a glamorous film
star. Even as he smiled from his great height and held out
his arms to me, I was rooted to the spot, afraid that if I
moved, the lights would come on and he would simply
disappear. He looked and dressed like no one I had ever
seen. Golden-brown light shot from his eyes, studded
above high cheekbones. It seemed that my grandmother's
face peered out of his. His white woollen cap with the
rolled brim sporting a peacock feather and his stylish
moustache gave him the elegance of an Indian film star
masquerading as a Mughal prince.

Moving toward me, he placed his hands on my shoulders and twirled me around. I was mesmerized by the agate-studded silver ring he wore on one finger. A fragrance rose from him, a combination of tobacco, shaving cream and throat pastilles. He murmured my name softly, adding the suffix *raani*, which means "queen" in Urdu. I fell in love with him instantly.

An unexpected visit from Amir, my mother's younger brother, was the greatest thrill in our home. Even my father avidly sought encounters with him. Although Amir had somewhat reduced financial circumstances compared to others in the family, he always arrived bearing exquisite gifts and rare delicacies from exotic places all over the country.

As a minor civil servant, Amir chose to be posted to remote mountainous regions, rather than the capital. Here he conducted official tours on horseback instead of by government car, wore indigenous clothes and disappeared for years at a time. With his flowing capes, he was a flower child long before it became fashionable.

At family gatherings, Amir's life story was often told through a series of indulgent speculations. While studying radio engineering in Bombay, in pre-Partition India, he was flooded with offers from Indian film directors to take screen tests. Yet his dazzling looks were never subverted by a hint of narcissism. He rejected the offers and returned to Kashmir, and in Pakistan, he married Shahida, a shy, gentle woman with pleasant features who was utterly devoted to him. She acknowledged the great affection my uncle showered on all of us with grace and generosity. With an uncompromising spirit, she endured the modest income and hardships of remote postings and adored her husband. I always thought she added ballast to his sails.

Her talents shone in sewing, although she also was a good cook. Her management of their homes was something of a miracle. Not only did she raise their seven children with very little help, but she tolerated the invasion of her kitchen by a husband who was a superior cook. In a culture where men of his background seldom cooked, Amir's skills were awe-inspiring. If he was available for family weddings, Amir even supervised the banquets prepared by professional chefs.

Amir had an obsession for ground chilies, and his consumption of cayenne was unparalleled. During family get-togethers he was known to leave the table and head for the kitchen. Cigarette clenched in the corner of his mouth, perfectly groomed moustache curled saucily at the ends, throat swaddled in a length of pashmina, he would squat on the floor and grind red and green chilies in a stone mortar. The entire family was convinced that something else was ground into the mix, as the consistency was thicker. But no one ever discovered what that something else was.

My grandmother, Dil-Aram, felt that Amir's excessive partiality for fresh chilies may have stemmed from his childhood. In Kashmir, circular cakes of spices and chilies, called *wardi,* were dried in the sun and stored in airtight containers for the long snow-laden months of winter. One small wedge added to a cooking pot would season the dish adequately. Yet when he moved to more temperate zones, Amir relished the opportunity to eat freshly ground chili pastes with his meals.

It was also speculated that he knew the bowl of chili paste resting by his dinner plate doubled as an elixir of health. Perhaps his stunning physical beauty and unblemished complexion were safeguarded by cayenne, which, laden with vitamins A and C, stimulates blood flow and dilates arterial walls so that nutrients reach their destination in the body.

Amir's visits to my parents' home were invariably marked by the ancient Mughal custom of presenting a gift, known as *nazrana.* How he managed this so effortlessly was part of his mystique. On one visit he gave my mother a goblet made of green stone and said that the minerals embedded in the stone had healing properties. I promptly drank water from it, convinced that magic coursed through my veins, and if I accidentally fell from the wild almond tree in the back garden, I would not break a single bone. Luckily, this belief was never put to the test.

On another occasion, Amir gave my father a small leather pouch fastened with a string. When he opened the pouch and the contents rolled out onto a serving plate, my father was speechless. Amir had brought guchi, a wild black mushroom as prized as truffles, which grows only in coniferous forests on hills at the great elevation of 2500 to 5000 metres. Such hills were easily found in the province of Jamu and Kashmir, now part of India, yet Amir somehow had found a source in Pakistan.

Guchi emerges above-ground in spring, and local folklore insists that rain, thunder and lightning must appear together to force the morels out of the mycelium plant. Hunting for the morels is an adventure, as gatherers never reveal their harvesting locations. Once they remove the morels, the plants beneath are permanently destroyed. The morels are later sundried, the cream-coloured base and black cap shrivelling up to resemble small pellets of crumpled leather.

Despite my mother's offer to cook the guchis Amir had brought, he carefully unbuttoned his shirt cuffs, rolled the sleeves precisely to his elbows and headed toward the kitchen. My father appeared stunned at the idea of a married man of Amir's social standing cooking a meal himself. He even protested to my mother, who simply ignored him. Amir returned an hour later, nodded briefly at my mother, unrolled his sleeves and carefully buttoned the cuffs. When the dish appeared at the table, the deep woodsy flavour of the morels had the texture of a fine beef tenderloin with an accompanying dark *jus*. I simply attributed this result to Amir's sorcery. Who else could convert a fungus into meat?

﹡

Much to the envy of my siblings, I once had private access to Amir for ten days. I was almost eighteen, and this experience offered new horizons for my adventurous mind. Ironically, Amir's home at the time was in a region that had inspired author James Hilton to write his book *Lost Horizons*. The days spent with Amir and his family centred around food and the challenging rituals of Mughal hospitality. They were also flavoured with generous bouts of rule breaking and hazardous outings.

The visit came about after I spent a year as a foreign-exchange student in the United States. On my return, I was indecisive about my university courses and spent a week in an apathetic bicultural funk. My canny mother suggested a trip to visit Amir, who at that time was posted in the Skardu Valley in the Northern Areas of Pakistan. I jumped at the offer, and the next day was seated in a small plane carrying me above the high peaks of the Karakorum range, some rising to eight thousand metres. K2 is the highest peak in the Karakorum range and the second highest in the world. The mountains encircle the town of Skardu. According to local folklore, the name Skardu is derived from the word *Iskaraldu,* the oriental name for Alexander the Great, who is said to have founded the town.

The Baltistan region, where Skardu is located, was under Buddhist rule in the eleventh and twelfth century. It was also the terminus of the fabled Silk Route, which brought silks from China and brick tea from Tibet to be traded for spices and salt. The Mongols and Chinese intermingled with local tribes in the region, giving birth to a regional cuisine with a strong emphasis on stir-fried meats. In the late eighteenth century, Kashmiris repeatedly tried to annex the area, as it adjoined their territory, yet were held back.

The game of polo flourished in this region. Although it originated in ancient Persia, where it was called *changan*, the name for the stick, the people of the Karakorum lay stronger claim to it. The Mughal emperor Akbar was so fascinated with the game that he played it after sunset with lighted balls.

A trip to Skardu meant that if there was fog over the huge mountain peaks, flights were cancelled. In my case, it was an act of good fortune that the fog appeared only on the day of my departure, leaving me stranded with Amir and his family for another five days.

On my arrival, Amir, dressed in an embroidered wool coat and Skardu cap, greeted me at the tiny airstrip. Empty apricot and peach orchards travelled beside us as we drove to his home in a jeep, for it was late autumn and the harvests had been picked in the valley. His tiny home was made of grey stone, local mud and mortar, with windows opening to the dark shadow of the mountains. A white stallion lived in an adjoining shed.

Inside the house, I was greeted by my little cousins, red cheeked and dressed in local woollen clothes like their father. Amir's wife whispered, "We all love you very much," and retreated to a primitive kitchen to cook dinner on the wood-burning stove. I followed her simply to watch. She prepared lamb with dehydrated vegetables. Because the valley was snowbound for a third of the year, summer produce was dried and stored. In her kitchen, I saw for the first time sundried tomatoes, which, unlike the Italian variety, swelled in the cooking fluid and regained the texture of fresh tomatoes. We ate dinner sitting on thick rugs on the floor around a raised wooden plank covered with a heavy tablecloth. Even the four-year-old was fed the highly spiced meal.

After dinner, I joined Amir in the tiny room that served as a sitting room. Local *namdas,* woollen rugs embroidered with pastel floral patterns, covered the entire floor, and cylindrical cushions lined the walls. I sat on the floor with Amir, and as the mountain wind howled outside, watched him brew cocoa for me in a miniature silver samovar. Perhaps he felt that I yearned for the beverages of the West, as I had just returned from a year abroad.

As I sipped the scalding cocoa, reduced in the continually boiling samovar to a stream of pure chocolate, Amir told me that the bowl I drank from was a collector's item. It had been produced in the Russian Gardner factory, referred to as *Gurthener* in the local patois, one of the three most important porcelain factories of its time. In 1746, Peter the Great granted permission to Englishman F. Gardner to manufacture his porcelain. Catherine the Great collected many pieces, and in 1891, the factory began making porcelain for the masses. The samovar was equally rare, but it was the taste of cocoa that lingers even today. I attribute my great love of chocolate and lifelong habit of indulging this taste in alarming proportions to Amir's delicious cocoa.

The next evening, Amir presented another delight in the sitting room, one that I kept secret from my parents for many years. In the tiny fire-lit room, swathed in a woollen cape embroidered at the collar, Amir pulled out a local stringed musical instrument and plucked the cords with his tapered fingers. On the floor in front of him were a little stone flask and two crude glass cups. He poured a red liquid into one cup and handed it to me, instructing me to sip it slowly, then resumed playing.

With my first taste, I thought I was drinking juice that had turned a little. Amir watched me with smiling eyes as I took another few sips, quickly draining the cup. He then informed me that I had just drunk the local mulberry wine. He told me that most cultures brew some form of alcohol, and it is always wise to sample local culture at all levels. In the face of this simple utterance, an entire spiritual taboo flew out of my life, for despite their liberal and permissive attitudes, my parents respected the ban on alcohol for Muslims and did not serve it in their home.

My ultimately sophisticated uncle made sure I knew that alcohol was also consumed in the country I lived in, and that it was meant to complement a meal as well as add a spirit of relaxation or celebration to social occasions. The great eleventh-century Persian poet Omar Khayyam, known for the sensuality and wisdom of his work, delivered more than a hundred quatrains of epicurean verse in which he used the singular metaphor of wine.

It seems that my family members frequently sought exceptions to rules. Many years later, during one of her rare visits to my Canadian home, my mother and I took a trip by airplane to the United States. When the flight attendant stopped the drink trolley at our seats, my mother looked at me thoughtfully and commented that a little white wine would add a festive touch to our holiday. I was so stunned that I promptly refused her offer.

⋞⋟

During my visit with Amir, the cherished principles of Mughal hospitality floated down four centuries in an outing he planned. He was taking me to visit the ruler of the neighbouring valley of Khaplu, because the ruler's sixteen-year-old wife spoke English and would enjoy my company. The hundred-kilometre journey would take about five hours by jeep, and we would ride the final mile on horseback. It was an official visit for him, he said casually, but I could wear trousers if I chose.

The jeep cut through a swath of terraced field, orchards and the meandering Shyok River. I sat with Amir in the back seat. He wore his *balti* wool cap rakishly tilted over his forehead, an oatmeal-coloured coat and a turquoise pin fastened at his throat. He chain-smoked throughout the drive and delivered a first-rate history lesson, occasionally offering handfuls of dried apricots as a snack. When we reached a cluster of men waiting for us with horses, I found that the mountain air had stimulated my appetite. Fortunately, we were to have lunch with the rajah of Khaplu. I rode to the palace on a silken brown mare called Bigli, which means "lightning," and Amir rode a black stallion, looking ready to gallop off and rescue a princess.

The short-statured rajah greeted us outside his wooden palace, a square building with a pyramidal roof crowned by a steeple. I was immediately escorted inside to a chamber where a pigtailed schoolgirl, wearing a wool sweater draped with a gigantic necklace of gold sovereigns, introduced herself as the queen of the breathtaking valley. When she asked me if I had brought any books written in English, I was devastated to have to say no. Living in a tiny village perched on the slopes of steep and inaccessible mountains, she yearned for contact with the outside world, and loneliness shadowed her delicate face. Yet centuries of royal etiquette prevailed over her personal desires, and she presided over an ornate silver tea service and offered imported English ginger tea biscuits with exquisite courtesy. I was a guest who had disappointed the young queen by arriving empty-handed, yet she served me refreshments with great charm.

When I was led away to have lunch, the young rani of Khaplu did not accompany me. I was taken to a long room where Amir, the rajah and three other men were seated on a carpet where a *dastarkahn,* or tablecloth, had been set with English china, silver cutlery and water glasses. I sat between the rajah and Amir. Platters of food arrived and were laid out in front of us. The central dish was a rice pualo cooked with meat. Unlike the biryani, in the pualo the meat, stock, rice and ground brown onions are cooked together.

As the rajah lifted a spoonful and served me, the powerful smell of fat assailed my nostrils. A wave of nausea gripped me, and I turned to Amir helplessly. He simply nodded to my plate and smiled. Within seconds, I was confronted by a heaping plate of rice dotted with chunks of lamb fat, a local delicacy. I watched in horror as my fastidious gourmand uncle lifted a forkful to his mouth and nodded his appreciation. I had yet to lift my fork. He quickly leaned forward and whispered in my ear, "Eat it. You are being honoured." I held my breath, lifted a forkful to my mouth and swallowed it with a gulp of water.

On this occasion, I learned that even the most unappetizing food must be eaten if one is a guest. The most elegant man in my family took me to a fairy-tale mountain kingdom to teach me this code of civilized behaviour. However, this incident also left me with an obsession for removing all traces of fat from lamb before cooking.

❧

My last adventure with my uncle occurred in a region of Pakistan known as Little Tibet. This dangerous trip created a mysterious link with a younger cousin and convinced me that emergency food portions should be included in every picnic.

One afternoon, Amir and I, accompanied by his eldest son, Shujat, went for an outing to Satpara Lake, a pool of emerald water ringed by mountains. In the middle of the lake was a tiny island, where we planned to have tea. A boatman rowed the three of us, accompanied by a picnic basket, to the island in a wooden boat. After dropping us off, he returned to shore, promising to return for us in two hours.

The picnic hamper contained a flask of tea and a tub of almond and semolina *halwa,* a granular dessert softened with cream and flavoured with nuts and floral essences. Amir had woken up early that morning and cooked the halwa himself. Sitting on the green shrubbery dotting the little island and chasing down mouthfuls of halwa with strongly brewed tea, I was introduced to Amir's penchant for unusual picnic fare. While I gazed at the dark mountains ringed like sentinels around us, he told me that according to local folklore, fairies lived on the island. I wondered if the inhabitants of Skardu had sighted fairies as a result of imbibing mulberry wine.

Suddenly a gale descended from the mountains, tugging at our clothes and sending the picnic hamper rolling. The wind churned the water of the lake, changing it from green to black and sending up large waves. Amir shouted across the lake to the boatman to come for us. The boatman, obviously terrified of the water, pointed upward and refused to move. Amir shouted himself hoarse for over half an hour without any results. I was terrified and my little cousin clung to me. After two hours, a young man appeared on the opposite shore. He spoke to the boatman, and together they lifted a large rock into the boat. The young man then rowed through the turbulent water toward the island. We watched his perilous progress with fear until he reached us.

Within seconds, Amir was in the boat and helping me and his little son into it. He made me sit, and seeing my rigid, fear-stricken face, gave me instructions. "Do not look at the water. Just look at my face and hold on to Shujat. If anything happens you are in charge of him. Never let him go." He lifted an oar and started to row, and with the young man delivered us safely to shore.

❧

On a family visit to Islamabad, Pakistan, many years later, after Amir had died, I met Shujat. He was now a general in the Pakistani army. During a family dinner, I reminded him of how superbly his father cooked wild mushrooms. In response, he offered to take me back to the lake where we had picnicked with his father.

Within two hours we were on a flight to Skardu, accompanied by Shujat's nine-year-old son. The lake was now graced with a little inn by its side, but it was still enchanting. After an afternoon filled with nostalgia for Amir, we returned to Skardu, only to find that fog had rolled over the mountains and the flight could not take off for Islamabad. I had to catch connecting flights back to Canada the following day, and so we set off immediately on an eight-hour drive through the Karakorum mountain range to the adjoining state of Gilgit, where another plane waited for us.

Because my cousin was a senior army officer, a small armed convoy accompanied us. There was no time to prepare a meal. Instead, the army cook packed four dozen egg sandwiches and a big flask of tea. Eight hours and twenty egg sandwiches later, Amir's son delivered me to safety. Roles were reversed. He said that he had considered me quite heroic when he was young, and I replied that he incarnated the spirit of Amir. We both felt that Amir's spirit had moved with us, and he was testing our resilience. What we did not know at that moment was that these tests would occur each time we met. Whether we simply wanted to keep his memory alive or were cursed with a sense of misplaced heroics, the trials always seemed to find us.

The last informal meal I had with my mother before returning to Canada was shared with my eldest aunt, Dilshad. My mother and aunt both had dietary restrictions, and so the food was moderately spiced. Small bowls of green chilies and mango pickle accompanied our meal. Watching me heap both pickles and chilies on my plate, Aunt Dilshad gave me a stern look and said, "I hope you are not going to behave like Amir."

Wild Black Mushrooms (Guchi)

This recipe can easily be doubled. To savour the dish, serve it with plain steamed rice or whole-wheat flour chapatis; combining it with heavier meat dishes will diffuse

the distinctive flavour. Black morels are expensive and
can be purchased at South Asian specialty stores.

2 tablespoons vegetable oil
1 pound black morels (guchi)
1 medium onion, finely chopped
1-inch piece fresh ginger, ground to a paste
4 cloves garlic, ground to a paste
1 teaspoon dried coriander powder
1 teaspoon black cumin seeds
1/2 teaspoon cayenne
2 tomatoes, blanched and puréed
1/4 cup water
1/2 teaspoon chopped fresh fenugreek
1/2 teaspoon garam masala
2 teaspoons chopped fresh coriander

Heat the oil in a large skillet over medium-high heat
and fry the morels until tender. Remove and set aside.
Add the onion to the pan and fry over medium heat
until dark brown and caramelized. Blend in the ginger,
garlic, coriander powder, cumin and cayenne; fry, stirring, for 1 minute. Add the puréed tomatoes and fry
for 4 or 5 minutes. Stir in the morels and water and
bring to a quick boil. Reduce the heat to low, then mix
in the fenugreek and garam masala. Serve garnished
with chopped fresh coriander.

Serves 4.

6

Aunt Shaad Serves Her Famous Fish and Kale

❦

We were entering the dragon's lair. The family car halted in front of a wooden gate, on which a small plaque with neat lettering read 29 C, Model Town, Lahore. The occasion was a rare visit and invitation to dinner at my aunt Shaad's home.

My parents were in great spirits because she had promised to serve a favourite Kashmiri dish, but my siblings and I were more subdued. All encounters with Dilshad Mahmud, called Shaad by the family, were fraught with tension. Her career as headmistress of a girls' school and, subsequently, education inspector of schools had seeped into her personality. Bad table manners, dirty fingernails, flying strands of hair, unbuttoned sweaters and the failure to eat every morsel on one's plate were subject to searing reprimand. Even the lavish gifts my mother had brought for her younger sister would lead to a lecture about wasting money, and my father would be rebuked for sanctioning this extravagance. My aunt's temperamental ferocity, the Spartan modesty of her home and the five-star cuisine she served were overwhelming for me as a young girl.

Aunt Shaad was married to a fussy academic who hid in a book-lined study, emerging on cue to save us from the consequences of her wrath. His endeavours were marked more by failure than success. She was also the mother of three sons whose academic achievements were legendary, as was their ability to create mayhem on all social occasions. Even their mother's draconian responses to their rebellion left them unchastened. From my vantage point, they were the bravest boys in the family, as they actually lived in the dragon's lair. They would retain this courage in the face of harrowing circumstances in their distinguished and unconventional adult lives.

I had the added burden of the knowledge that when I was born and my mother fell ill, it was Dilshad who took care of me for a few weeks. Therefore, I felt obliged each time I saw her to offer proof that I had been worthy of her endeavours. I did not know at the time that Shaad longed for a daughter of her own. Many years later, this yearning led Amir, her dazzling younger brother, to leave a daughter in her care for a few years.

Unlike other members of my family, Aunt Shaad would jot down recipes with precisely measured ingredients in lined exercise books. The rest of her siblings considered this a sacrilege. After all, they were the children of Dil-Aram, from whom they had inherited the highly mysterious yet celebrated trait of cooking by memory. No one, of course, had the courage to challenge Shaad's meticulously handwritten recipe books. I was certain that she could have governed a small nation and prepared dinner for a hundred single-handedly.

Aunt Shaad lived in a modest brick bungalow in the city of Lahore. On entering, I was immediately struck by the shining cleanliness. Every object in the home was dusted to perfection. After a fierce embrace, she instantly asked me about school and where my latest report card placed me in my class. While the rest of my family wandered toward the pre-dinner delicacies laid out on the table, I braced myself to deliver a lie, prompted by the rapid disappearance of the guava salad to respond expediently. My mother flashed me an indulgent smile and rescued the last of the salad from my marauding siblings. Dilshad "the Dragon" narrowed her eyes and led me to the dining table, where she sat me next to her. My heart sank because I knew that along with her superb food would come further interrogation, and

I would have to be careful, above all, not to place an elbow on the table.

A large platter with fillets of white fish resting in a tangle of kale appeared on the table, bringing ecstatic smiles to my parents' faces. A flame-coloured sauce lapped at the edges of the green, creating perfect contrast. My aunt served me, with a warning to look for fish bones, as it was impossible to completely debone the fish without tearing the flesh. A reverential hush descended over the dining table, and I lifted the first forkful to my mouth. I could not identify the combination of flavours—all I knew was that I liked the taste and could finally understand my parents' excitement.

When I acquired the recipe years later, I realized that the fish had absorbed the flavour of the kale and the spices, and yet it retained a hint of sweetness. Nuggets of black cardamom, normally removed from a dish after cooking, dotted the sautéed kale. Apart from watching for bones in the fish, I had to be careful not to bite into the black cardamom, as it released an intensely pungent flavour. This favoured Kashmiri dish, a gastronomical triumph laced with hazard, was a perfect metaphor for my aunt's personality.

During that visit to Aunt Shaad's home, I learned why my parents yearned for this particular Kashmiri dish. Karachi, where we lived, neither delivered fresh river fish nor grew kale. Yet the paeans sung to this dish were also part and parcel of my family's gourmand temperament. They seized a specific pleasure and heightened its enjoyment by imposing on it a heavenly status. To my family, cuisine had the same prominence as art, literature or music, and skilful preparation of food was a creative process that was not to be taken lightly. Pleasure was transcendent as well as fleeting, and thus it was meant to be celebrated immediately.

When my parents tasted the fish and kale, it was as though they were listening to a favourite Verdi aria. My father's eyes became moist, and the compliments he heaped on my aunt were excessive and positively maudlin. In turn, Dilshad "the Dragon" snorted dismissively, as if she had placed a fried egg on a plate and my father had mistaken it for caviar. Beneath her gruff exterior, my formidable aunt had an intrinsic modesty.

❧

Kale is as essential to the Kashmiri diet as potatoes are to the Irish. It is braised or steamed and added to fish, meat and fowl. This ancient headless cabbage, a bouquet of large dark green fibrous leaves, dates back two thousand years to the Greek and Roman civilizations. It also packs a nutritional punch by delivering calcium, potassium and vital antioxidants to the body.

Any firm-fleshed white fish can be used to prepare fish and kale, such as cod, sea bass, monkfish or even shark. Rao and mahasher, caught in the Ravi River, are used in Lahore, located on the east bank of the river. The name Lahore comes from Loh, son of Rama and hero of the Hindu epic the *Ramayana*. Sikh and Hindu dynasties ruled Lahore before it became part of the Mughal empire from 1524 to 1752. Both the Mongols and Turks were drawn to the fertile plains, where grains, vegetables and fruits grew in lush abundance.

During their reign, the Mughals secured the city by surrounding it with a nine-metre-high brick wall. A rampart with a circular road gave access to the city through twelve gates, which were closed at night. The gates led to specific areas of the city; one area is still called Mughalpura after the Mughals. The Mughal emperor Akbar built a large fort, which emperors Shah Jahan and Aurangzeb later extended. The Badshahi mosque, Shalimar Gardens and tombs of both Emperor Jahangir and Empress Nur Jehan continue to breathe life into the Mughal presence in this city.

Two districts of Lahore were heralded for their prepared food in Mughal times, and still are today. In Gawalmandi, slabs of rao and mahasher fish were cooked in a spice-laden batter and served with gigantic flat-breads. Clay ovens grilled meats and fowl to perfection, and huge vats of freshly made yogourt sat next to steaming cauldrons of a Punjabi dessert called *rabrdi*.

Shahi Mohalla, meaning the "royal area," was known

for a section called Hera Mandi, or the "diamond market." The diamonds were the famous courtesans of Lahore, who served perfumed condiments on betel leaves, recited verse, danced *kathak*, the Mughal court dance, and selectively accepted the patronage of men.

One particular food, beef trotters, enjoyed the same notoriety as the courtesans of Hera Mandi, and the inhabitants of Lahore continue to trek to the area in quest of this dish. Beef trotters, or *paya*, are cooked with spices until a hearty gelatinous stew evolves. The flesh, marrow in the bones, gelatinous broth and naans or rice used to mop it all up exact a penance from the digestive system like the ponderous elephant cavalries of the Mughals did from their enemies. When the elephants advanced, the ground shook and the enemy trembled, yet the emperors perched in the *howdahs*, decorative seating booths, had postures of invincibility. In mere mortals, the lining of the stomach distends, the heart beats slowly, the tongue is coated with spices, worries disappear and the gait slackens—the only solution is to take a nap. The possibility that this dish had roots in a courtesan conspiracy to tantalizingly delay sexual pleasure while the gastronomical delight was digested, raising the ensuing material reward, hints at the power of food. In a sense, food creates an invisible dialogue that can be more effective than speech.

I learned of the power of food to change minds first-hand when, three decades after my first taste of fish and kale, I cooked Aunt Shaad's famous dish at a Kashmiri dinner party. I was visiting childhood friends in Lahore, and my host fancied himself a chef extraordinaire. An assimilated Mughal himself, his ancestry was always suspect as far as I was concerned because it travelled beyond the Mughal empire to Europe. His mother was French, and he grew up in a home where French and Pakistani cuisine were served at the same table. My Kashmiri heritage was the subject of affectionate banter between us. Yet Jeanot Jahangir Malik, also moonlighting as the honorary French consul in Lahore, had to be silenced, and food was my weapon of choice.

I kidnapped Lasoo, still part of our family, to supervise my preparations. He was like a high priest grudgingly giving sanction to a junior acolyte's attempt to emulate a sacred ritual. When I accidentally broke a fillet, Lasoo struck his chest as though I had plunged a dagger in his heart. Moon-faced Jahangir subsequently broke all genteel eating records by consuming at least three portions of fish and kale and offered a peace plan for our ongoing cultural war.

❧

Aunt Shaad's power lay in her ability to cook superb food without the bravura showmanship and emotional excesses of her siblings. The dishes at her table resembled a mosaic, each course seamlessly complementing another. Even the filled water glasses were lined in identical places near each dinner plate. Her culinary management, whether it was at her home or in a relaxed outdoor setting, was adaptive.

If she were a reincarnated Mughal, she would be Emperor Akbar, who built a new city at Fatehpur Sikri in India. To prevent himself and the city residents from being deafened by the sounds of stone and wood cutters, he ordered that all materials be shaped elsewhere and then brought to the site to be fitted together. Shaad, while preparing *karela,* a dish of stuffed bitter gourds called *chirnits,* did not simply wrap string around the gourd. Instead, she took a threaded needle and sewed the gourd along the opened seam. The thread was later pulled out simply by tugging on one end, and the stuffing never spilled out. Yet although Emperor Akbar was championed for his benevolent rule, my aunt evoked awe bordering on fear in her extended family.

My mother adored her younger sister Shaad and expressed great admiration for a woman who combined marriage, children and an exacting career with fortitude. She had also home-schooled her three sons for a brief period when her husband was posted to the small town of Rawalakot, in the Kashmir region located in Pakistan. She opened a girls' school in that town at the behest of the president of the region.

Both sisterly love and intellectual affinity flourished between my mother and Aunt Shaad. My mother often told me that Shaad's kitchen was a temple of hygiene and order. Her table service was simple and austere. There were no flowers or decorative linen on the table, for excellent cuisine stood on its own without enhancements—all that was needed was a good appetite. Unlike my mother, my aunt used cooking tools that were labour intensive but more than sufficient. A good saucepan, a sharp knife and the appropriate cooking temperature were all that she required to prepare any dish, anywhere. There was also a holistic bent to her cooking. She used oil and the infamous cholesterol-laden ghee sparingly and would immediately send a dish with a layer of grease on its surface back to the kitchen to have the oil skimmed off.

Aunt Shaad's exacting personality concealed a loving heart. Family accounts reveal that when Dilshad took on her mother, the exquisite Dil-Aram, the ensuing clash of the titans led my grandmother to indulge her daughter by acquiescing. One such conflict, which I had only heard about, concerned the recipe for a dish I was convinced was bits of towel thrown into a stew.

Lamb tripe cooked in a Kashmiri kitchen is transformed by the addition of three ingredients. My grandmother added two green herbs, fenugreek and dill, yet Dilshad insisted on adding spinach as well. I first tasted the dish at my aunt's home when I was a teenager. I took a large serving and found the first mouthful intriguing. Unlike a cube of lamb or chicken, which has a consistent texture, tripe is smooth and rubbery on one side, and the other is covered with springy fibres sprouting out like a soft brush. When I asked which part of the animal this meat came from, my graphic imagination revolted and I could not continue eating. I was certain that Dilshad would view this transgression unfavourably, so I busied myself hiding pieces of tripe under the pile of rice on my plate and eating forkfuls of gravy instead. Yet I wondered what would happen when I reached the portion of rice that concealed the tripe underneath. Would this escape Aunt Shaad's eagle eye?

What transpired a few tense minutes later won my undying respect for Aunt Shaad and filled me with the wondrous notion that dragons too can have tender hearts. Looking me squarely in the eye, she informed me that in future I should restrict my helping to one spoonful, in case I did not care for the dish. Then the waste would be minimized. She lifted my dinner plate and set it aside. Then she looked at me thought-fully, and said that as a child I had possessed quite an appetite and could be fed anything, and I had looked like an apple in the wool caps she knit for me. They were pixie caps with two pointed ears—did I remember them?

Returning home from that family holiday in Lahore, when Aunt Shaad had served her famous dish of fish cooked with kale, I was jubilant on two counts. First, I had not been reprimanded once for bad table manners, and second, Aunt Shaad had not really been left behind. Waiting for me was a brown paper parcel, my name care of my father written on it in black ink script. Even the post office bent to Dilshad's will, as the parcel had somehow made it to our home before us. It was covered with beautiful local stamps and fastened with a sturdy white string. The string was quite unnecessary, as the homemade glue sealing the paper tested the mettle of my scissors. In fact, the parcel was designed to survive monsoons, post office pilfering and unseemly haste.

Eventually, I unwrapped a square tin box lined with waxed paper, offering neat lines of her famous walnut toffee made with *gurh,* pure unrefined sugar. Battles were fought over Dilshad's toffee. My sister, Mahjabin, would hoard her share in the third drawer of her dresser under a pile of scarves. My brother, Shahid, and I would sniff it out like bloodhounds and polish it off. The punishment of writing three hundred lines of "I will not eat my sister's sweets without her permission" was a price worth paying. Each caramel-coloured square melted in the mouth immediately to reveal the moist, milky young walnuts inside.

My last visit with the inimitable Shaad was in 2003, at her home in Lahore. Ravaged by ill health, she chased innumerable caregivers from her bedside when they failed to measure up to her standards. Her two sons conducted interviews worthy of the Gestapo to prepare the local nurses for their mother's exacting care.

Despite my aunt's shockingly weakened bedside embrace, I controlled my shattered response, because I knew that she would not tolerate any show of sympathy. When tea was served accompanied by chocolate cake from a local bakery, I cut a thin wedge for myself. The family dragon rose from her pillow and fiercely reprimanded me for cutting a small piece and demanded to know whether I was dieting. I had no choice but to polish off a third of the cake to allay her suspicions.

Her eldest son, Tahir, entertained me during this visit in an attempt to cheer me up. Tahir was known in the family for tracking the movements of the last great Kashmiri *wazas,* "chefs," in Pakistan with the same enthusiasm he had for hunting the endangered ibex. The great chefs are dying off, he would moan, yet nobody really cares. He often ate dinner in his bedroom and flouted his mother's conventions by hosting dinner parties with at least half a dozen meat entrees. With Kashmiri charm, he convinced his guests to overeat. He exercised the same charm to convince a friend who had cultivated a Kashmiri waza to bring cooked Kashmiri food with him on the flight to Lahore. He also courted female *ghazal* singers, arranging lavish soirees with large quantities of red wine, despite living in a country with state-sanctioned prohibition.

One evening he invited my sister and me for dinner at a restaurant in Lahore that had various food kiosks resembling Pakistani villages. In the confusing array of over a hundred dishes, we singled out the *paya,* or lamb trotters. Within ten minutes, a mountain of lamb bones rested on my sister's dinner plate. The combination of my cousin's devastating charm, which made him encourage my sister to keep eating a dish she relished, and my sister's gluttony resulted in a middle-of-the-night visit to the emergency room of a hospital, where indigestion was mistaken for a more serious medical crisis.

But it was with Aunt Shaad's youngest son, Tayab, settled in the United States, that I discussed our family history. In our telephone conversations we inevitably waxed nostalgic over some family dish we were both pining for at the moment. I also knew that he was pining for a mother he had not seen in a few years. We would tantalize each other with descriptions of the food our mothers served. Sometimes the anguish trickling through the telephone lines led us to create the dish, and our next conversation would ring with triumph. However, unlike our Mughal ancestors, we had yet to devise a way to transport food between the borders of Canada and the United States.

A few months later, when my mother told me that Dilshad, who regarded her failing health as a nuisance and probably the height of bad manners, had perished in an uncharacteristically quiet fashion, I felt as though a stabilizing force had left my family in Pakistan. Unable to attend her funeral, I spoke to my mother and all her siblings on the telephone. When I condoled with my cousin Tayab, our conversation ranged from family history to Kashmir and finally, in an attempt to override our grief, a discussion of how his canny elder brother, Tahir, once flew to reclusive Aunt Dilkhush's home merely to have lunch. Here, the spirit of Dilshad resurfaced. We could picture her serving some mouth-watering delicacy and a blistering reprimand on extravagant long-distance telephone bills on the same plate. Aunt Shaad probably also would have reproached her younger sister Dilkhush for indulging Tahir's extravagant food cravings.

Fish and Kale (*Machli Saag*)

This entree can be served with steamed basmati rice and a light lentil side dish. Use a dense fish that will hold up while the kale cooks—in Canada, whitefish is a superb variety. The fish does not require lemon, as the tomatoes and the kale naturally add tartness. When arranging on the platter, simply allow the kale to lie as it falls from the serving fork.

One 1-pound firm white-fleshed fish, such as cod,
   monkfish, shark, whitefish or sea bass, filleted
1 medium onion, thinly sliced
4 tablespoons mustard-seed oil
2 medium tomatoes, diced
2 small dried red chilies, crushed
4 cloves garlic, ground to a paste
1-inch piece fresh ginger, ground to a paste
2 pods black cardamom
1 teaspoon black cumin seeds
1 bunch fresh kale, washed and trimmed
Salt to taste
1/2 teaspoon garam masala

In a large skillet, fry the fish lightly on both sides merely to seal in moisture and firm the pieces. Set aside. In a deep, wide pot, fry the onion in the mustard-seed oil over medium heat until dark brown and caramelized. Stir in the tomatoes, chilies, garlic, ginger, cardamom pods, cumin and salt to taste and sauté until the mixture becomes a smooth paste, about 10 minutes. Reduce the heat and carefully place the fish fillets on top. Arrange the kale over the fish and sprinkle with salt. Cover the pot and cook over low heat until the kale wilts and becomes tender, about 30 minutes. Halfway through the cooking time, rearrange the kale so that it is coated with the sautéed spices beneath the fish, and sprinkle garam masala on the top layer. Arrange the cooked dish on a platter using a wide, wedge-shaped spoon, taking care not to break the fish.

Serves 3 to 4.

My grandmother, Dil-Aram Sirajud-din Ahmad Dar

My grandfather, Khan Sahib Sirajud-din Ahmad Dar

BASHIRABAD, SRINAGAR, KASHMIR

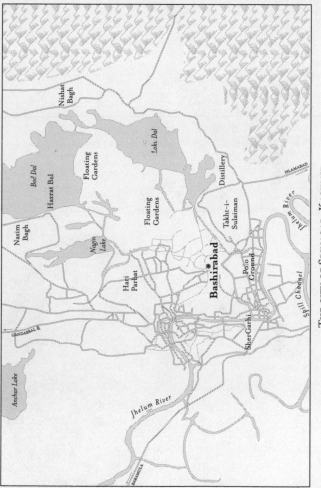

THE CITY OF SRINAGAR, KASHMIR

My mother,
Dilafroze Anwar Sheikh

My father,
Mohammad Anwar Sheikh

UNCLE AMIR

Uncle Amir and family, Skardu, Baltistan

AUNT DILSHAD

Aunt Dilkhush

AUNT DILNAWAZ AND HER HUSBAND,
MAJOR AHSAN-UL-HAQ BUTT

AUNT DILARA

UNCLE BASHIR AND AUNT AKHTAR

Lasoo

Author (third from right) with siblings and cousins

7

A Secret Recipe from Aunt Khush for Kashmiri Hareesa

'TIS ALL A CHEQUER-BOARD OF NIGHTS AND DAYS
WHERE DESTINY WITH MEN FOR PIECES PLAYS:
HITHER AND THITHER MOVES, AND MATES, AND SLAYS,
AND ONE BY ONE BACK IN THE CLOSET LAYS.
—Omar Khayyam, *The Rubaiyat*

❧

I can still remember that scorching July afternoon when I lay covered with a cotton sheet on a hard settee. A ceiling fan revolved overhead, ruffling the edges of the peephole I had constructed by winding the sheet around my face. I was spying on my aunt Khush, who reclined on a couch at the far end of the cavernous living room in her Islamabad home. In her deceptively mild voice, she had told me to take a nap and stop fidgeting, and my sixth sense told me to be obedient.

This was my mysterious delicate aunt who wore her hair in a coronet of braids, suffered from debilitating headaches and was generally found reclining on couches.

Sometimes as a cure for the headaches she bound a length of georgette tightly around her forehead, giving her the appearance of a gypsy, and remained undaunted by my fashionable mother's objections. Aunt Khush was also a formidable chef, who like my mother would not permit anyone to enter the kitchen when she was cooking.

After polishing off white radish cooked with dried mango powder, black lentils and mounds of steamed rice, my mother and another aunt, Dilnawaz, dressed in cool summer muslins, had disappeared on a marathon shopping trip to purchase the trousseau for a cousin's wedding. Dilkhush, which means "one who makes the heart happy," shuddered at the thought of hitting the bazaars in the heat of the afternoon. I had been left behind to keep her company while she rested in the cool living room behind drawn curtains, with small fans positioned on end tables.

The afternoon nap was the most lethal of all restraints forced on me by adults and one my mother practised with devastating regularity right up to the time I was a teenager. It became a form of instant imprisonment, release coming only with the rattle of teacups announcing that evening tea would be served. I did not have the courage to tell Aunt Khush that I would have much preferred to leaf through her photograph albums lying in the heavily embossed walnut bookcase.

In the front hall of her home was a framed photograph of her taken many years ago that I found mesmerizing.

The stunningly beautiful face capped with gleaming dark hair and luminous eyes tilted upward bore but a fleeting resemblance to the woman stretched on the sofa. Sometimes I thought that she must be an impostor, and the real aunt in the photograph was lost somewhere, waiting for me to discover her. So I lay motionless, keeping one eye on her as I pretended to be asleep but daydreamed about climbing the mulberry trees laden with crimson and white juicy berries in her garden. Sleep was the furthest thing from my mind as I calculated how many steps it would take to tiptoe past my sleeping aunt.

Ultimately, I lacked the courage to skip the nap and raid the mulberry trees, and instead I waited restlessly for Aunt Khush to wake up. When she finally rose and asked me whether I had slept, my garbled response led her to burst into soft laughter. At that moment, I saw in her a marked resemblance to the woman in the stunning photograph.

Compared to my other four aunts, Aunt Khush had a tantalizing secrecy to her, probably as a result of her life experiences. She alluded to one dramatic event on the odd occasion but provided a frustrating lack of details. Even my mother adopted a distracted air, as though this difficult subject was best left alone. Despite my curiosity, all I succeeded in establishing was that Dilkhush's double wedding with her elder sister, Dilnawaz, or Naazi, as she was called by the family, took place amid the civil war. Her plans to travel to the glamorous city of Bombay with her husband were sadly derailed by the turmoil of Partition, and instead they took what turned out to be a perilous six-day journey through a hostile land. The destination was her husband's family home in the city of Lahore, in a country that was barely three months old. This was all that was said of the mysterious event, and I simply regaled myself with images of ornately dressed Kashmiri brides who had taken the wrong fork in the road.

Many years later, on a visit to Pakistan, I saw Khush and finally heard her own account of the flight with her sister Dilnawaz from Srinagar to Lahore during Partition. Even in this harrowing tale, food played a principal role. The two brides, Dilkhush and Dilnawaz, accompanied by their husbands and a handful of relatives, boarded a wagon bus that they had rented to take them to Lahore. Within a few hours of their journey, there was talk that Hindu and Sikh pursuers followed them. The bus driver abandoned the passengers halfway through the journey at a rural village, on the pretext of engine trouble. In fact, he was a Hindu, and he worried that if he were caught transporting Muslims he would be killed.

The wealthy landlord of the area knew that the two brides were the daughters of Khan Sahib Sirajud-din Ahmad Dar and escorted the bridal party to his ancestral home in the town of Ramban, India. His ancestral enclave turned out to be a cluster of mud homes. Khush and Naazi were unaware that a bloody civil war raged throughout both countries. Naively, they thought their husbands had taken them on a rural honeymoon. Each day, their hosts brought them freshly churned buttermilk in clay pots and lentils, mustard greens and spinach accompanied by corn flour rotis. Later in life, mustard greens became a sought-after delicacy for Khush.

Over the next three days, the brides frolicked with their husbands in the surrounding forests, carrying makeshift picnics to escape the barren mud homes. However, within twenty-four hours their Eden was invaded by the grim realities of the civil war. On the second night a young Hindu girl from a neighbouring village sought refuge with them. In the middle of the night the landowner arrived demanding the girl, but the bridal party refused to hand her over. Yet the next day the girl returned to her village without consulting them.

On the third day the group decided that as no transportation was available they would start walking. They abandoned the bridal trousseaus on the roadside, tossing aside the suddenly frivolous silk garments and beautifully embroidered table linen. After they had walked a mile, the bridal party was accosted by tribesmen from Pakistan's North-West Frontier, headed to rescue Kashmir from India. They mistook Khush's darker-complexioned brother-in-law for a Hindu and held him. To convince

the men that they were in fact Kashmiri Muslims headed
for Pakistan, the entire bridal party recited verses from
the Koran.

Eventually, Khush's brother-in-law was released and
the group continued walking, until suddenly they saw a
pile of corpses in the road ahead. The men went to
examine them and found the body of the young girl they
had hidden for the night. When Khush and Naazi saw
the shocked faces of the returning men and asked ques-
tions, the first awareness of the horrors of civil war
filled them with terror. Both brides then removed their
wedding jewellery, which their husbands hid in the rolled-
up waistbands of their trousers. Khush recalled that when
her brocade wedding shoes were at the point of tearing
open, a Pakistani military convoy appeared on the road,
headed in the opposite direction. After the soldiers interrogated them, a young major took pity on the two beautiful brides and put the entire wedding party in his army
truck, driving them to safety in the town of Rawalpindi.

In Rawalpindi the sisters split up. Naazi and her
husband headed for the town of Jehlum, and Khush
and her husband took the train to Lahore. When they
reached Lahore before dawn, the house of mourning, for
the family had assumed they had perished, was instantly
transformed by great jubilation. Although it was almost
dawn, the groom's family immediately prepared a highly
festive wedding dessert. The Punjabi dessert *zarda,* a

medley of rice, cream, saffron, almonds, raisins, pistachios and lime juice, was the first meal Khush consumed in a new homeland, whose borders remained sealed from Kashmir. Khush considered the timeless Mughal tradition of marking life's auspicious moments with a "sweetened mouth" an omen of good fortune.

※

In my large food-obsessed Kashmiri clan, we were always told in advance what dishes were to be served, as a way of extending for hours the delights of anticipation. But Khush was the exception. She refused to discuss her menus, reminding me of a puzzle box where hidden chambers would reveal themselves only if the right pressure were applied at the appointed spot. She used this element of surprise as an effective tool, especially in presenting her astonishing forte, the labour-intensive Kashmiri *hareesa*, a dish that no one else in our family would undertake to prepare. Her bravery in this regard only confirmed my suspicion that her indolent physical style was a decoy.

In Srinagar, hareesa was cooked through the night and sold in the teashops in the morning because it took so many hours to prepare. The cook used a technique called *gothna*, applying intense pressure to the meat with a cooking implement such as a spoon or a wooden cylinder. Aunt Khush did all of this herself.

Petitioning for this dish was always an onerous task for the family. Kush would note the request and then prepare the dish without any notice, extending casual invitations to her siblings, my aunts and uncles, to dine with her. The magical appearance of the dish rendered her guests speechless. It was as though the peacock throne built by Emperor Shah Jehan were placed in front of them, and all they could do was gasp. She served her guests individually, disappearing into her kitchen and then reappearing with a bowl full of boiling hareesa, garnished with crisply caramelized onions in ghee. We had to wait patiently while the food cooked, for she heated each portion individually in metal bowls, then wait again for the hareesa to cool down.

Khush never discussed her method or recipe, and it became a family tradition to land up at her doorstep and hope that hareesa would be served. Khush knew her relatives well and indulged them by presenting the dish faultlessly on many occasions. She exhibited a weary disdain for all the compliments parcelled her way, implying that everyone around her was an imbecile to even consider that she could fall short of establishing herself as the mistress of this dish in our family. If the recipe were altered in any fashion what would emerge would not be hareesa. It was as simple as that.

This dish reflected a large part of the history of the Mughal empire. Freshly slaughtered lamb was used, a meat that Kashmiris prized above all others. The grazing lands of northern India were also ideal for raising this animal. The dish was a combination of meat and kernels of wheat cooked for many hours. Although hareesa was the product of an amalgamated cuisine, it was the Kashmiris who adopted it, used authentic ingredients and excelled at making it. Grain was a portable ingredient for the Mongols, who were the first to invade India. The Mongolian men on horseback used their spiked helmets as cooking pots and stumps of wood as stirring utensils. The velvety texture of hareesa could have been the result of both the lengthy cooking time and the stirring utensils, for the stumps of wood were ideal for mashing and breaking down the fibres of the meat.

The Persians, masters of cultural refinement, relied on the element of delicacy in art, cuisine and decorative motifs. As a result, Kashmiri hareesa is a dish that is both robust and delicate. The cracked wheat kernel adds a robust fibre, and the pounded meat has a fibreless transparency to it. The spices, with the exception of black cardamom, are lighter ones. Another Persian touch is the garnish of dried fenugreek leaves, less pungent than fresh, sautéed in ghee. The other garnish for hareesa is a pencil-thin kebab of ground meat, a Turkish and Afghan influence. Kebabs of ground lamb or beef sculpted into balls and threaded on skewers for the grill are to Turkish and Afghan cuisine what the hamburger is to North America.

In the hands of the Persians and the Kashmiris, sauces and gravies were added, creating dishes called *kofta, gushtaba* or *rista*. Other versions include the *nargisi koftal,* which opens to reveal a boiled egg inside, and the Persian meatball, studded with golden sultana raisins, combining savoury and sweet. The Punjabis substituted lentils for wheat and used beef and chicken, calling it *haleem,* the Gujaratis of India almost liquefied it and called it *khichra,* and Parsees added pumpkin, eggplant and potatoes and called it *dhansak*. Yet there was collective reverence paid to the Kashmiri hareesa, which was foie gras compared to the chicken liver pâté of the other regional concoctions.

The obsession with altering texture may have been influenced by the textile weaving techniques of the time. Sumptuous brocades, embroidered fabrics, silks and cottons were so finely woven that they became diaphanous, and cuisine followed the same principles. Sheets of silver were hammered until they weighed less than a butterfly's wings, then draped over food as edible decoration. Scented floral waters were added in the final stages of cooking. Serving dishes and platters lifted architectural shapes. The Mughal arch or dome, the lotus flower and the unopened buds of pomegranate trees were incorporated into design and even affected the language of the day. The word *Mughlai* in cuisine became identified with a definite style that included visual artistry with culinary finesse.

❧

As an adult, I always visited my aunt Khush when I returned to Pakistan. I would casually land at her doorstep, and my spontaneity would be rewarded by a silent but passionate embrace. A small procession of dishes would appear, served by Khush herself. Conversation flowed endlessly between us. I suppose in many ways I had been conducting lifelong interviews with her. I felt that despite her indolent posture, she lived life fully, and her outward appearance was a subterfuge of sorts.

She always employed young women as helpers in her kitchen and trained them exquisitely, for although she was married with two sons, her domain was essentially female. Her husband, a mild-mannered banker, treated her like a delicate flower that should be left undisturbed. Unlike the kitchen in my mother's home, which resounded with a cacophony of cooking sounds, hers was a silent floating space, and my imaginative antennae quivered in readiness to interpret some word or gesture that would reveal more about her. At times she would unexpectedly release her coronet of braids and let her waist-length black hair flow unfettered. As she offered me fennel seed mixed with shredded dried coconut as an end-of-meal digestive and leant back on the sofa, she reminded me of the women painted in Mughal miniatures, reclining with flasks, vials and platters of fruit ringed around them, their faces lost in contemplative reverie.

It was at one such tranquil moment that Khush decided to share her life experiences with me. For the first few years of her married life, she had lived in a joint family system. This system meant that a bride lived in the home of her husband's parents. If the home was large enough, married children were encouraged to live there until they were established and could buy or build their own homes. There were conflicting opinions of this social practice. Tyrannical mothers-in-law dominated households by making the young brides of their sons reside in humiliating submission. My aunt reversed the experience, converting it into a valuable apprenticeship in food management, and regarded the multi-storey home as a small hotel where even breakfast was customized for each person she served it to.

Each week her mother-in-law would hand over the kitchen to one daughter-in-law. So Dilkhush, along with the kitchen helpers, planned, cooked and served the meals to the four families residing in the large home. Both her brothers-in-law had soft-boiled eggs for breakfast cooked to specific timing. Dilkhush took pride in being able to serve the two-minute egg and the three-minute egg on their respective trays.

Facing me squarely one day, she informed me that cooking was the ultimate act of love. She had moved from her hometown of Srinagar, and her siblings were scattered in various parts of Pakistan. She had also been traumatized by the horrors of the civil war on the flight to Lahore. Her in-laws were sensitive to her estrangement and showered her with affection, and the only way she could show her appreciation was by pleasing them at the table. She believed that cooking with love had the power to transform food. Even a simple lentil could become a banquet delicacy if it was cooked with love.

Khush's interest in cooking was sparked by the variety of foods prepared in her in-laws' home. She won over her in-laws by including the Kashmiri repertoire from her own childhood home. Her ongoing courtship with her husband also revolved around food, and when it was her week to manage the kitchen, she prepared special dishes to please him.

Her recollections of her childhood home, Bashirabad, were filled with loving anecdotes of both parents. The legendary Dil-Aram, her mother, appeared to her as a beautiful woman who wore fine clothing and jewellery and ringed her eyes with kohl. Like her other siblings, she had no recollection of her mother ever teaching her to cook. Khush had no memories of even seeing her mother cook or go shopping for food.

As a child, she observed that a special lightly spiced cuisine was prepared for her father, and the vegetables served to him became some of her own favourites. Her father told her that black pepper was regarded as having medicinal value, especially for the tonsils. She also accompanied him on short trips to the town of Sialkot, where her father served her food himself. The man who intimidated his entire household and had given her the attribute of "one who makes the heart happy" also indulged in a unique relationship with her. When he fell from a horse and hurt his shoulder, young Khush would lace up his shoes for him, and she knew from memory which pocket he placed his reading glasses or handkerchief in.

After Khush married, it was her mother-in-law who encouraged her to experiment with cooking. Her own mother merely cautioned her to cook with a light touch and issued only one reprimand, and that was for using too many walnuts in a favourite Kashmiri chutney.

The Kashmiri walnut chutney was eaten inappropriately in our family, according to Khush. Apparently, some family members viewed it not as a condiment but as almost a vegetable entree. Her condemnation of those who committed this folly was scathing: people who overate the chutney were in essence mules. On her list of family mules, her brother, the dazzling Amir, with his equally scandalous addiction to ground chili paste, was right at the top. When the walnut and radish chutney was presented at her table and I sparingly served myself a tablespoon, and then glanced at her nervously, in a moment of rare indulgence she nudged me in the ribs, laughed and moved the bowl toward me.

To make this chutney, large white radish is ground with fresh walnuts and fresh red chilies. The chutney is not pounded into a paste but only partially ground, leaving a coarse texture and small fragments of walnut. The flavour of this condiment is unique, as it bears no resemblance to the usual chutneys made with the favoured coriander or fresh mint leaves. It is also typically Kashmiri because it includes a nut.

The walnut chutney, in fact, should have been served as a vegetable entree of sorts to be eaten in whatever quantity one chose. Yet in the mysterious mind of Dilkhush, the specified order of cuisine was not meant to be disturbed, even in the case of a lowly condiment. Through restraint at the table, one displayed a superior intelligence that would prevail over vulgarity. Piling a mound of walnut chutney on a plate with other food would indicate that some inadequacy of flavour had been detected in the other courses. This could be observed by the host and create distress. Dilkhush's philosophy of consumption was based on an intricate etiquette, with the purpose of giving pleasure. This attitude was shaped by the grand Mughal etiquette itself, but like Aunt Shaad she adhered to it with a certain rigidity that added a sombre touch to the table.

One of Khush's startling confessions has haunted me from time to time, because I felt as though she had stumbled on my own secret. Her confession, delivered apologetically and almost in a whisper, was that she preferred her own cooking to that of others. Unlike Aunt Shaad, she saw my request for recipes as quite amusing. When I asked her to wait until I found pen and paper, her response was initially disconcerting. Measured ingredients were the wrong approach, she cautioned me. Seasonings had to be adjusted, as meat and vegetables had varying rates of absorption. Handfuls and pinches were the terms she used, while I had trained myself to use measuring spoons and cups.

In her opinion, cooking absent of two qualities was doomed to failure. The first was love, and the second was *andaaza,* which means "estimation." When I asked her to explain how one learned andaaza, she responded that although it was indefinable, it was largely a matter of practice. She said that food memories coiled in the brain mysteriously and could be resurrected at will. Determined not to be waylaid by her enigmatic responses, I asked her what one would do if the estimation had gone wrong and the dish was a failure. She replied that it had to be set aside and prepared again with new ingredients. I told her about my life in Canada, where I cooked alone without any help in the kitchen and could not possibly have enough time to make two versions of the same dish. She skewered me by asking why I had allowed myself to be distracted the first time. Did I, like her younger sister

Naazi, hold a book in one hand and stir a pot with the other? Finally, she added, signalling an end to the conversation, there was no school or chef who could either illustrate or teach one how to incorporate these two elements in cooking. Either they existed or they did not. It was always as simple as that for a woman who served unforgettable food.

Kashmiri Hareesa

Serve this dish with whole-wheat tandoori naan, either unleavened or yeasted. No side dishes are required. At the end of the meal, serve platters of sliced oranges, for according to my aunt Dilkhush, they aid digestion.

4 pounds boneless lamb
1 head garlic, ground to a paste
6-inch piece fresh ginger, ground to a paste
2-inch-long cinnamon stick
1 tablespoon black cumin seeds
2 teaspoons finely chopped red chilies
1 teaspoon black peppercorns
Salt to taste
12 cups water
2 cups white rice
2 cups cracked wheat, soaked in 2 cups water for
    1 hour and drained
3 tablespoons garam masala
3 tablespoons dried fenugreek

1/2 cup ghee (clarified butter)
1 cup caramelized onions

In a large pot, place the lamb, garlic, ginger, cinnamon, cumin, chilies, peppercorns and salt. Pour in 6 to 8 cups of the water and boil over medium heat for 2 hours, until the fibres of the meat separate. Cover the pot partially with a lid and tip it to drain off the water.

Meanwhile, in another large pot, boil the rice and cracked wheat with the remaining 4 cups water until it reaches the consistency of a porridge, about 45 minutes. Stir the meat mixture into the grain porridge. Cook over low heat for about an hour, mashing every 5 minutes with a sturdy, oversized wooden spoon, and adding a cup or two of water as needed to create an opaque and smooth texture. When the individual consistencies of grains and meat are indistinguishable, the hareesa is cooked.

Sprinkle the garam masala on top, cover with a lid and steam for 3 minutes. In a small skillet, fry the dried fenugreek in the ghee for 1 or 2 minutes. Transfer the hareesa to either a large serving bowl or individual bowls, and garnish with the fried fenugreek and caramelized onions.

Serves 6 to 8.

8

My Favourite Aunt Naazi's Delicious Kebabs

HERE WITH A LOAF OF BREAD BENEATH THE BOUGH
A FLASK OF WINE, A BOOK OF VERSE—AND THOU
BESIDE ME SINGING IN THE WILDERNESS—
AND WILDERNESS IS PARADISE ENOW.
—Omar Khayyam, *The Rubaiyat*

My aunt Dilnawaz and her husband, Major Ahsan-ul-Haq Butt, had just moved to a new home and invited the entire family to visit. The army had posted the major to the town of Nowshera in the Mardan district, south of the historic city of Peshawar, gateway to the Khyber Pass. Aunt Naazi welcomed us with fierce embraces, rocking us while crooning endearments into our ears. Her name meant "the hospital heart," but everyone called her Naazi. She was tall and voluptuous, with dark flashing eyes and a rose tucked dramatically behind her right ear like an Eastern cabaret artist.

When she told us that *chapli kebabs,* a specialty of the

region, would be served for dinner, my brother and I were filled with curiosity. The word *chapli* meant "sandal" in Urdu, and we wondered if our unconventional aunt would feed us footgear masquerading as food. Our imaginations ran riot, and Aunt Naazi was like a geyser spraying us with laughter and merriment. All the children at the dining table were hypnotized by her, for to us she was more a peer than an adult.

Aunt Naazi rose from the table and announced that the new cook was one of her husband's military orderlies, and she wanted to make sure he cooked the kebabs to her specifications. Her husband bestowed her with a besotted smile. My father glanced at him and said that the army should use his favourite sister-in-law's effervescence as a morale booster. My mother simply beamed at the antics of a younger sister she adored and did not get to see often.

On the centre of the table sat a water tumbler jammed with fuschia roses. Their petals were opened in the limp splendour of full bloom, and the powerful scent tickled my nostrils. The sound of crickets, the warm night breeze and the spit curl in the centre of Aunt Naazi's forehead brought ambience to the stark dining room.

Her table was covered in a dark green plastic tablecloth that I found intriguing. I had never seen a plastic one before and thought it had magical properties. I dropped a dot of red chutney on it and then removed it with my fingertip. There was no stain left behind, and I wondered naively if my mother had noticed this. Spilling food on her immaculate white tablecloths at home resulted in the famous "look." She never issued a verbal reprimand, but instead instantly registered the carelessness with a rapier-sharp glance, causing in me a tide of despair from head to toe. Even though the moment was fleeting and she looked away, I felt as though I had let the entire universe down. But tonight I was in the charmed domain of my jovial favourite aunt, Naazi, who made sure my mother would have no reason to flash the "look" at anybody.

Laughter rang out from the kitchen, accompanied by sizzling and a delicious fragrance that seeped into the dining room. A man wearing khaki trousers and a matching shirt carried in a large china platter of food. Naazi followed him, clasping a straw platter with a stack of naans close to her chest to preserve their heat. We passed the platter around the table, filling our entire dinner plates with gigantic elongated discs of ground meat, marked with crisp brown lines from the grill. Slivers of red tomatoes, green coriander and chilies and yellow-and-white egg glistened through the steam rising from the kebabs.

To make the kebabs, an enormous black steel disc was heated to a searing temperature then spread about half an inch thick with seasoned ground lamb or beef, filled with crunchy coriander and pomegranate seeds. The kebab cooked within four minutes and was then seared on the other side. It was a dish that reflected the history of the region. The Pathans of Pakistan were known for their rough-and-tumble social etiquette—even their regional dances were fierce and war-like. One theory held that the kebab was called *chapli,* meaning "sandal," because the wild west Pathans stamped on the ground meat with their feet, like the grape crushers of Italy. Luckily, I only learned of this bit of cuisine trivia many years later. Had it been aired at the table on that memorable night, my finicky thirteen-year-old temperament would have prevented me from doing full justice to Naazi's magnificent chapli kebabs.

Naazi was the younger sister of Khush. Together, as new brides, they had fled Kashmir through Partition-ravaged India to Pakistan. I could not imagine Naazi weeping for a moment over her torn brocade wedding shoes. I saw her racing from the forest on bare feet, a mane of tumbling hair flying on her shoulders, outdistancing all her pursuers. It was fitting that by some quirk of fate her husband had been posted to a region with a history as dynamic as her spirit.

❧

The Mardan district is part of the North-West Frontier of Pakistan. This province was once considered the gateway to India and always had a reputation for being ungovernable. The Pashto-speaking tribesmen were expert marksmen and daring equestrians. They created their own laws, refused to part with their cultural norms and roamed freely, protected by their tribal allegiances.

The first recorded invasion came from the Chinese kingdoms, bringing Buddhism to the area. Then came the warring Afghan kings, who considered the region their backyard. The Persian conqueror Nadir Shah travelled through the area to sack Delhi, accompanied by his most accomplished commander, Ahmad Shah Durrani, who built an empire in neighbouring Afghanistan. This was followed by the territorial mandate of the Sikh ruler Ranjit Singh, who annexed the region until the Mughals invaded and secured it. In the fifteenth century, the Mughal emperor Babur arrived through the Khyber Pass, and in 1581, Emperor Akbar built the historic Attock Fort to fortify the Afghan frontier.

The Kabul and Indus rivers sweep through the region, and the town of Nowshera sits on a sandy plain on the banks of the Kabul. Although the rivers yield two varieties of fish, rao and mahasher, both are used sparingly in the local cuisine. The region's cooking is largely based on grilled meats, for the harsh terrain, accessed by passages hacked out of mountains, is remarkably devoid of heavy forests and fertile agricultural land. The local game, duck and black partridge, are grilled as regional delicacies. Duck is also marinated with spices and cooked slowly with onions, yogourt and garam masala. A turmeric and water wash dispels the game odour.

Despite the construction of a few hotels, government resthouses and widened roads, the people have retained their tribal culture and still build fires for heat and to cook their traditional meals. More refined cuisine has not spread to this last frontier. Kebabs of cubed or ground meat line the outdoor grills of marketplaces and home kitchens. Black partridge impaled on the tip of a Pathan dagger and roasted over coals still surpasses the meats cooked in the more sophisticated clay oven, the tandoor. The accompanying simple salads are a confusion of onions and tomatoes drenched in vinegar.

Dishes also are cooked in the *kardhai,* a shallow-bottomed steel pan with handles on the side, resembling the Chinese wok. Chinese influence is reflected in both cuisine implements and architecture; it is believed, for example, that the famous Mughal Attock Fort was built over a Chinese palace. The refining touches of Persian cooking, however, are nonexistent in this cuisine. In this area, with its long-standing reputation of aggression, foods are grilled and seared within minutes, as though at any minute a battle might erupt or an invader might pound at the gates.

❧

Aunt Dilnawaz took to the posting in this region enthu-
siastically, becoming fluent in Pashto and learning to
cook the local dishes. Yet in the ultra-conservative Pathan
culture, where women covered their heads and even wore
the veil, Naazi refused to buckle under convention. As a
partial concession, she donned a pair of dark sunglasses.
Major Ahsan's wife may have raised eyebrows by loitering
in bazaars with her head uncovered, as she purchased
skewers for grilling kebabs, but she won over her Pathan
friends with her Kashmiri cuisine. In her mind, our visit
to her new home meant we should sample the local
cuisine, so she included grilled kebabs in most of the
meals she served to us.

During that brief stay at Naazi's home, I also learned
that apart from cooking, my aunt had a passion for
reading. Naazi devoured novels in English and Urdu.
She would wake up in the morning, kiss her dashing
husband goodbye, get her children ready for school and
then head to the kitchen and cook throughout the
morning, preparing the meals for the entire day. When
she finished, she would retire to her room and read all
afternoon, while smoking cigarettes and downing cups
of Kashmiri tea. Her absorption in the novels was so
intense that her children, husband and household help
had been trained to leave her undisturbed. Many years
later, she confessed that she cooked with speed and made
many dishes together to allow enough time to catch up

on her reading. She inhabited the worlds of the novels she read, taking great pains to inform us about plot lines and characters without realizing that she herself could easily have been the heroine of a family saga.

Blessed with a cheerful disposition and a degree of fearlessness, she became a model army wife. Just before Partition, she had dropped out of university to marry the young army captain, who was fifteen years older than her and worshipped the ground she walked on. Like the marriage of my parents, theirs was a love affair that survived parenthood and some tragic life changes. Naazi and Ahsan were lovers, best friends and relaxed parents, which was unusual in an authoritarian society.

During postings to remote areas she assembled a household immediately and always appeared at the dinner table dressed, perfumed and sporting roses in her hair. As a woman, Naazi was not modern or emancipated; instead, she seemed to come from a romantic era when women expressed themselves without fear of censure. In temperament, she could have easily matched the Mughal empress Nur Jehan, who shot tigers from the howdah of an elephant but also created a fragrance known as attar of rose, or she could have been a throwback to the eldest daughter of Emperor Shah Jehan, Jahanara, who oversaw the construction of many public buildings and held titles normally reserved for men.

At one stage of her life, Dilnawaz built a home in the city of Rawalpindi and supervised the construction site herself, battling with contractors and land tax departments. She brought bundles of cooked food to the building site, surprising the workmen with a lunch of kebabs folded into naans. She also had superb instincts for finding outstanding food, searching out local specialties as a symbol of her willingness to embrace a new and bold frontier.

❧

A decade after that memorable visit with Aunt Naazi in Nowshera, I returned to the region for my eldest niece's wedding in the city of Peshawar. My favourite aunt, whom I had not seen for a few years, was expected to attend. The entire family gathered under the same roof: a state guest house that had been the Pakistani lodge of the deposed King Daud of Afghanistan.

My Pathan brother-in-law, who had once courted my sister in a red Cessna over Karachi skies, had resorted to unparalleled showmanship and reserved this lodge for his wife's Kashmiri clan. In the gigantic front hall, two staircases spiralled down from the second floor. Apparently, custom dictated that the king and queen descend from separate staircases. Upstairs, an endless corridor was marked by rows of doors leading to mammoth bedrooms. Amid a cold winter in

Peshawar, the family was billeted in this unheated magnificence.

Naazi's response was to immediately hold a secret meeting in her bedroom. Here she held court wrapped in duvets on her bed, a dog-eared novel, ashtray and box of cigarettes at her bedside. A tray of breakfast, carried up from the kitchen and down the mile-long corridor, sat untouched, for the congealed omelette and cold toast with a waxen smear of butter had failed to engage her appetite. The enormous fireplaces in the bedrooms were not lit, and the staff remained purposely vague about lighting them.

It was distinctly possible that Naazi would rise from her cocoon, march us to the garden to hack down a tree for firewood, and cook kebabs in the fireplace. However, she announced that as a distraction from the freezing lodge, we would take a clandestine trip to the famous Khyber Pass, where excellent Kabuli pulao and *seekh kebabs* could be obtained. The kebabs and the rice pulao of the region were distinguished by their meat and seasonings. She had chosen a handful of lucky people to accompany her on the trip, so my sister and brother-in-law would not suspect that some of us were missing. With her elder sisters present, Naazi hoped her absence would go unnoticed.

The road to the Kyber Pass was a fifty-kilometre stretch, beginning just west of Peshawar. The route cut through the Hindu Kush Mountains and was patrolled by Afridi clansmen, who regarded the pass as their private reserve on the Pakistani side. Beyond Torkham, the Afghan frontier was patrolled by Shinwari tribes of Afghanistan. Within a few metres of the main road, both Pakistani and Afghani law gave in to tribal law, and visitors travelled with armed escorts.

Although there were no Chinese, Persian, Greek and Mughal invaders to fear, the folklore attached to the Khyber Pass lent excitement to our excursion, which would last a couple of hours and bring us back in time for the evening's pre-wedding festivities. We piled into the car on the pretext of a shopping trip, Aunt Naazi sitting in front with the driver. Within half an hour, we had left the city behind and were headed up the winding road toward the pass. We saw plumes of smoke rising from tiny homes cut into the mountainsides. Buses carrying bearded tribesmen sped by. The forest of rifles resting against their shoulders, leather straps of ammunition holders woven across their chests and turbans with the ends draped across their faces set them apart from people in the rest of the country. Surprisingly, in deference to the local culture, Naazi covered her head with a shawl and wore her husband's army-issue sunglasses.

Army posts, checkpoints and memorials to British regiments carved on the rock face sped by as the car raced toward our first destination. Shepherds with flocks of sheep dotted the mountain pass, and clusters of nomads walked on narrow pathways. We saw no women. Our first stop was the little town of Landi Kotal. It had a long-standing tradition of being a smuggler's town, where weapons, electrical goods and the silks of China were sold at unbelievably low prices. However, food was the objective of our trip, and Dilnawaz guided the driver to a kebab stand. A man pulled long cigar-shaped seekh kebabs off skewers, slapped them on sheets of newspaper and handed them to us in the car, along with green-glass bottles of Coca-Cola. The ground-beef kebabs were riddled with fat to retain moisture while the meat cooked. We chased down the fiery seasoning of the kebabs with gulps of fizzy cola. The sensation was of having ingested gunpowder, which travelled down the barrel of a hunting rifle. The flavour was unforgettable and the man who brought food to the car was armed to the teeth.

Our final destination, the settlement of Torkham, was a few miles away at the border of Afghanistan. Torkham greeted visitors with a low cluster of build-ings, housing customs, immigration and checkpoints, protected by an enormous barbed-wire gate. The tiny settlement clustered together as though it found security in being close. It was exciting to imagine that beyond the heavily patrolled gate lay the city of Kabul.

There were small shops and restaurants in the area, but Naazi had warned us that we would remain in the car for the duration of the trip. The car halted near a small open-air restaurant. Another bearded and armed man approached the car, and Dilnawaz spoke to him in Pashto. The man ended the conversation, calling her "sir" in English, giving a little salute and walking away. Within ten minutes, he was back carrying a gigantic tray piled with tin plates of rice pulao—rice cooked in a meat broth and studded with carrots, raisins, chickpeas and chunks of meat. No cutlery was offered, so we scooped up the pulao with our fingers. The meat was lean and stringy, but the raisins and carrots added moisture and a touch of sweetness, which even the cumin could not alter.

The history of this dish could have come from the pages of the Indian history textbook I studied at school. In the border town of Torkham, Mughal kings with Afghan allegiances were bested by wily Persians, and Mongol horsemen cantered through Kandahar headed for central India. Tribal allegiances had brought this dish from Afghanistan to the North-West Frontier of Pakistan, where it was adopted as regional cuisine. This history lived on through the flavours bursting in each mouthful of Kabuli pulao.

Our appetites sated, we easily forgot the unheated rooms of the royal lodge, even when Naazi instructed our driver to make for Peshawar at record speed. During the drive she listed the spices that flavoured both the kebabs and the Kabuli pulao, just in case we were inclined to cook the dish ourselves at home.

⚘

Even after I moved to Canada, my enchanting aunt Naazi never left my side. I had a constant need for news about her. The patriarch of the family, my mother's elder stepbrother, Bashir, sent me albums of photographs taken at family gatherings. In his mind, I may have been the niece who had left Pakistan for Canada, but I was not to forget the family. The odd photograph of Naazi at some family gathering was reassuring. Her stance dominated the more demure poses of her sisters, and she had replaced the spit curl of another era with an unruly lock of slanting hair.

When life exacted a nightmarish toll from her, I was shocked but knew she would endure. Her husband died and her only son succumbed to a degenerative ailment. During visits to Pakistan, I saw her at family functions and was always amazed to find that her essential spirit remained unaltered. She still loved laughter and food, and she would lampoon members of the family, cigarette in one hand and novel in the other, remaining invincible until the day she suffered a severe stroke. My mother's sorrow-filled voice on the telephone providing details of the damage made me feel as though I had stopped breathing. Unable to deal with this reality, I simply placed my faith in hope. My laughing, dancing aunt was up to any adventure tossed her way, and she would recover and continue to cook.

Toward the end of that year, I planned a short visit to Pakistan to see my mother and counted the days till I would see my aunt, who then lived in the town of Rawalpindi. My mother had warned me that Naazi was not her old self. At that moment I felt like a university student living in residence who had come home to find her bedroom rearranged by her mother. I called Naazi's daughter and told her I would be visiting soon.

On a crisp late spring morning, clutching a mass of roses from the local bazaar, I landed at my aunt's home. She was sitting on the front lawn in a wooden garden chair, a brilliant shawl embroidered with flowers and birds draped across her shoulders. Next to her was a small table with a book and a glass of pomegranate juice. Her back was turned to me, and as I circled the chair calling her name, she turned around with a lopsided smile. I was given a sudden seated embrace, the roses crushed between us. The mane of hair framed her face, where I could see traces of the damage caused by the stroke. She raised one eyebrow and pushed a rigid smile from two-thirds of her face. Placing a finger on my lips, she conveyed the message that I was not to focus on the ravages. Then she played the buffoon and made a few faces for me. I selected a rose and pushed it in her hair, now threaded with silvery strands.

Naazi informed me that she knew I was coming and had ordered some of my favourite dishes, including a dessert. The pomegranate juice in the glass had been pressed for me. When she said the word *meetha,* which in Urdu meant dessert, she closed her eyes and adopted a dreamy posture. In that instant, I realized that she had an affinity for sweets that I had never known about. Then she drew a single cigarette from the folds of her shawl and asked me to light it for her. As I sipped the pomegranate juice, she convulsed with laughter and informed me that she had bribed her cook for the cigarette, dodging her caregiving elder daughter's restrictions. There was no force that could have prevented me from offering a light to my incomparable aunt.

Her stroke-damaged left leg did not prevent her from later entering the kitchen to peer at the cooking pots and demand fiercely why a garnish had been omitted. She asked the cook to see if there were any walnuts in the house for radish chutney. Lunch was to be spinach and lamb served with plain basmati rice. A plate of chapli kebabs was brought to the table, and she apologized for not making them herself. The dessert, which she decorated seated at the table, was a Mughal variety of bread pudding called *shahi tukra.* She also dispatched a servant to bring back plain paans, fragrant, condiment-laden betel leaves that I had learned to eat with her, and winked at me. We both knew that the wink meant she was thinking of my mother, who had never been partial to paans, believing they discoloured the teeth, and had banned them during my childhood. In Pakistan, there was also a tradition of adding opiates to paans, and that is why she used the word *plain*.

⚜

My last visit to my aunt's domain took place under different circumstances. I was in Islamabad visiting a cousin, who had cooked a welcoming banquet. After tasting every dish, I staggered off to bed with a heavy stomach. The meal was a combination of Kashmiri and Punjabi dishes, but I wished it had been simply Naazi's famous grilled kebabs. I prided myself on having a cast-iron stomach, and despite my discomfort was more concerned about next morning's visit to a military hospital, where an ailing Naazi had been admitted for a checkup. I would spend an hour with her before catching a flight to Lahore, and I wanted to tell her that I was using a cast-iron frying pan in my Canadian kitchen to cook chapli kebabs.

I spent a restless night waiting for the morning, aware that it was not indigestion but anxiety that kept me up. Dawn was accompanied by a telephone call from Uncle Bashir, informing me that Aunt Naazi had died late at night. Most of the family would reach Rawalpindi by noon, so he planned the funeral for that afternoon. Hours later I stood before a flower shop, holding sheets of roses, which are draped over coffins in Pakistan. Adjoining the flower sellers were sweet shops. The fragrance of flowers and sugar coiling through the congested area made me feel as though Aunt Naazi stood by my side. I was carrying with me a copy of my second novel and had wanted to see her face when I gave it to her. For one unbearably poignant moment, I wondered if I could convince Uncle Bashir to slip the book into Naazi's rose-laden coffin.

Chapli Kebabs from the North-West Frontier

Chapli kebabs can make an entire meal, served with naans or whole-wheat flour chapatis and yogourt sauce with shredded cucumber or a coriander chutney. Potatoes cooked in cumin and mustard seed make a good vegetable accompaniment. However, in a meal of multiple courses it is best to serve the kebabs as the first dish. Chapli kebabs also can be barbequed, but make sure the grill is coated lightly with vegetable oil. Never give the recipe of the chapli kebab to invaders.

2 pounds lamb, finely minced
I medium onion, finely chopped
2 medium tomatoes, finely chopped
4 green chilies, finely sliced
2 eggs, fried and chopped

1 tablespoon vinegar
Salt to taste
2 tablespoons whole coriander seeds
2 tablespoons pomegranate seeds

In a large bowl, mix the lamb with the onion, tomato, chilies, eggs, vinegar and salt. In a food processor, roughly grind the coriander and pomegranate seeds. Stir into the lamb mixture. Wash hands and squeeze the meat and ingredients together for about two minutes. Season a large cast-iron skillet or a shallow steel wok sparingly with vegetable oil and place over high heat. The skillet is ready when drops of water sprinkled on the surface instantly sizzle and disappear. Take a large lump of the seasoned meat and place it in the centre of the pan, pressing it out toward the edges. The kebab should be at least 6 inches long and 4 inches in diameter. Sear for 3 minutes, then turn it over to cook 3 minutes on the other side. Serve immediately.

Serves 4.

9

A Lamb Delicacy to Impress Aunt Dilara's Suitor

AWAKE! FOR MORNING IN THE BOWL OF NIGHT
HAS FLUNG THE STONE THAT PUTS THE STARS TO FLIGHT
AND LO! THE HUNTER OF THE EAST HAS CAUGHT
THE SULTAN'S TURRET IN A NOOSE OF LIGHT.
—Omar Khayyam, *The Rubaiyat*

❧

With a cupped palm my uncle gently patted my head twice, the word *beta,* or "child," rolling out with affection and amusement. He handed me an oval box of lemon drops. I could already feel my teeth biting down hard on the confection and my mouth flooding with the sweet-tart syrup. I said, "Thank you, Mamu-jan," meaning "uncle of my life," and withdrew, as my brother was next in line. Instead of a pat on the head, he received a handshake. Our parents, seated together, beamed at us.

Our living room had taken on a serene and dignified air, for my eldest uncle, Bashiruddin Ahmad Dar, was visiting us in Karachi. He was a broad-shouldered, imposing man dressed in a long waistcoat and swathed in woollen mufflers. Unlike our father, he combined East and West in his attire. The top half was Western, but his trousers were the Pakistani *shalwar,* a ballooning drawstring trouser ending in a narrow cuff. His English brogues were laced up tightly and polished to a high sheen. He had a receding hairline and wore large spectacles, which magnified his eyes. Beneath his penetrating gaze, I wondered if he knew that all I wanted to do was dash away and open the box of sweets.

My mother, addressing her stepbrother as Bhai-jan, "brother of my life," presided over a magnificent tea. Samosas, miniature kebabs, crustless sandwiches, Pakistani sweets and a lemon cake from a European bakery were arranged on a double-shelved tea trolley, which was wheeled around the room. Tea napkins embroidered with daisies, demitasse spoons and tea forks rested on the second shelf. I saw respect and exquisite hospitality reflected in the brilliant sparkle of silver and the gold-edged rims of my mother's best china.

My uncle held a position of great importance in the extended family. Bashiruddin Ahmad Dar was regarded as representing my late grandfather's wishes. He was the elder stepbrother of eight siblings, and my grandmother Dil-Aram always treated him as the eldest child of her family. This led him to adopt the role of family patriarch and behave like a visiting dignitary, who elicited the most courteous behaviour from those in his presence.

Although he had studied law, after Partition in 1947, Bashir held various posts in the Pakistani government to do with revenue and tax collection and administration of agricultural lands. He could tell us where the best rice or wheat was grown in Pakistan, or whether sugarcane juice was pure or adulterated by additives. His profession dealt with accountability, and he carried this responsibility into the family arena, regarding his colourful and passionate stepsiblings as wayward children who required constant monitoring and counselling. He was singularly aware of their ability to flout convention, make heroically doomed life decisions and even disregard his counsel. In the face of this, he always maintained an unruffled composure. Akhtar, his wife, sometimes comically subverted his control within their home, and behind his awe-inspiring facade, he also had a twinkling smile and was full of surprises.

⚜

Unlike his younger stepbrother, the irresistible Amir, Uncle Bashir made regular appearances in my life. My familiarity and love for him grew as I witnessed his life in his own home, where we visited often. On one memorable occasion, he summoned the entire Kashmiri clan to his home in the town of Campbellpur, Pakistan. My youngest aunt, Dilara, was being courted by a suitor who would come to dine and then formally ask for her hand in marriage. My mother and her sisters had been summoned to either intimidate or dazzle the suitor, depending on how they felt about him. It was an old family trick—in my uncle's strategic mind, just the display of splendour would be enough to repel or spur an advance. *Shebdeg,* Kashmiri turnips and lamb cooked in ghee, was to be served for dinner, and this dish would act as a tool of seduction and negotiation.

After we arrived the next morning, I wandered into the dining room. A large metal container shaped like a milk canister sat on the dining table. My uncle Bashir dipped a long-handled metal spoon into the canister, bringing out a waxy lemon-coloured fluid. He tasted it, pursed his mouth, peered into the canister and nodded. This was his stamp of approval for the ghee that would be the cooking medium for the special dinner.

Ghee is clarified butter that has been processed until all moisture evaporates. This process gives it a longer shelf life and allows it to be heated to higher temperatures, so foods can be fried or sautéed without burning. The canister on the table had just arrived from a village where a private dairy catered to my uncle's exacting tastes. The arrival of the ghee and its sampling to determine its purity were a ritual laden with tension, for my uncle had been rumoured to express his disapproval of the ghee through outrage that left even the stout-hearted trembling. He was not a person to trifle with, yet his wife, standing behind him, rolled her eyes and flashed a sardonic smile. Akhtar's comic disregard for my uncle's tasting ceremony filled me with admiration. It was as though a butterfly had entered the lion's den and flitted away with gossamer wings intact.

The approval of the ghee appeared as an auspicious omen for the start of the day in a home I considered a bit of a monstrosity. The facade was of red brick, with three Doric columns adding a touch of confusion. Enormous bamboo blinds protected the front of the house from the heat but gave it a forbidding look. The front veranda led into a huge central courtyard, where the kitchen also spilled out. The huge living room was dominated by a portrait of my grandfather wearing a Turkish fez, which used to hang in my grandmother's home. The ground floor also held the inner sanctum, my uncle's bedroom-cum-study. There were rumours that the shelves and desk drawers of this study were packed with important family papers my uncle had brought from Kashmir. No invitation had ever been extended to examine the papers, even though a large part of my grandparents' history rested in them. However, it was reassuring to know that Uncle Bashir was the custodian. Upstairs on the second floor was a maze of bedrooms with a few bathrooms sprinkled in between. There was a mysterious third floor where no one was encouraged to venture.

Mealtimes in this home sometimes had two sittings: one in the dining room for the adults, and the other in the vast living room for all the nieces and nephews. Dozens of eggs would be split open for Pakistani omelettes, and carrot and almond preserve would be served on dinner plates instead of in bowls. My father often teased my mother that her brother could feed an entire village at a moment's notice.

The light of this family was my uncle's wife, Akhtar, a short, rotund woman who wore horn-rimmed glasses and an enormous diamond stud in the right side of her nose. She laughed her way through life's vagaries and was considered the party girl of the family. Twenty houseguests did not alter her disposition. She was a daring and imaginative cook who remained undaunted by her husband's rigidity and introduced a relaxed campfire ambience whenever she could. Often she chose to serve dishes that required ingredients unavailable in the small town of Campbellpur and relied on substitution, creating her own versions. She displayed the same confidence in her sewing, cutting a jacket as expertly as she would debone a leg of lamb.

Akhtar was also the sophisticated bride from fashionable Bombay who discovered that her honeymoon was in fact a trek on horseback through the Northern

Territories. She promptly folded the delicate silks of her trousseau, donned a Solar Topi, a stiff-framed sunhat, and poured herself into riding jodhpurs and boots to ride alongside her husband while singing sad Indian love songs. Like my aunt Naazi, she did not have an authoritarian manner with children. She indulged personal whims instantly. If it was a rainy day and someone had a craving for *kardi,* chickpea flour dumplings infused with turmeric yogourt sauce, the dish would appear at the table with all the others she prepared. On occasion, she would hurl colourful invective at her domestic helpers, then collapse with laughter. No objection ever arose because they knew she could be relied on to protect them from my uncle's stern disposition.

To my mind my uncle unjustly received a certain amount of bad press, for he also played the family's grocer by supplying large sacks of fine basmati rice and wheat flour to his mother and stepsiblings. He also created a family fort, almost a country seat, where each member of the large Kashmiri clan was assured of hospitality. He chose the home in Campbellpur as land compensation from the Pakistani government for family property lost in Srinagar in 1947. His choice of location hinted at the inner grandeur my grandfather was known for. It was as though my uncle had decided that both the Indus River and Mughal relics had to be close at hand. Irrigated lands delivered fresh produce, and there was abundant grazing land for cattle. Wild duck and black partridge provided game meats. Thus, his table did not lack for anything.

Campbellpur, at the convergence of the Indus and Kabul rivers, has a colourful history. The area is renowned as the birthplace in 520 B.C. of the mathematician and grammarian Panini, who created the structure for phonetics, phonology and morphology in Sanskrit. In 1581, Mughal emperor Akbar, advancing into central India, passed through the area and built a fort and the first boat bridge across the Indus. Emperor Jahangir's wife, the formidable Empress Nur Jehan, designed and built a caravanserai in this region. While my uncle considered the nearby Tomb of an Unknown Dancer an architectural enigma, he regularly chose the serai pavilion, cooled by the winds blowing from the Indus River, as an appropriate setting for a picnic tea.

Because of its strategic position, Sikhs and Afghans fought with the Mughals over control of the area. In 1819, after the fall of the Mughal Empire, the Sikhs ruled until they were defeated by the British, who used Campbellpur as an artillery camp during their occupation of India. The Pakistani government subsequently changed the name to Attock.

I felt that my uncle wished in some modest way to add the history of our family to the region. In this home, he created files and ledgers tracking the movement of all our family members. He was always consulted about marriages, selling of land, selecting educational paths, divorces and scandals and had an impressive reputation for finding solutions, seated behind his desk in the bedroom. As the favoured witness for all family weddings, he was also the subject of many humorous anecdotes. During Muslim wedding ceremonies, the family witness secured the bride's signature on the wedding contract. One family bride, overcome by emotion, wept endlessly, delaying the wedding and thoroughly scandalizing my uncle. He promptly put her signature down in his own writing and rushed to deliver the contract to a bride-groom on the verge of nervous collapse.

Therefore, it was no coincidence but a matter of family tradition that Aunt Dilara's curly-haired suitor would dine that night at my uncle's home. The incomparable beauty of Dilara's saucer-sized eyes and the prized Kashmiri dish of turnips and lamb would be the bewitching elements of conquest. The sizzle of romance revealed itself with the disappearance of my aunt. She spent the entire day submerged in a bath filled with fragrant oils. It seemed that all of a sudden this aunt, who hiked with us and taught us how to tie a reef knot, became a languorous creature. The second floor of the house was transformed into a Mughal harem and was banned to the boisterous teenagers. My mother and her sisters disappeared upstairs carrying garments and jewellery, and a maid brought up a black metal clothes iron filled with coals. Trays of food periodically were sent up, as well. Clearly, some intensely female and private rituals were being conducted.

My uncle's wife immediately provided diversion for the cluster of restless children, ranging from toddlers to teenagers. Aunt Akhtar organized an alfresco lunch of fried puris and chickpea and potato curry. We ringed around her, plates in hand, watching circular discs of flour puff up into little translucent balloons in the enormous iron skillet as they were deep-fried. Lunch was followed by pistachio *kulfi*, a Mughal version of ice cream set in clay cones sealed with salted flour. The clay cones were placed in a large clay pot filled with ice and continually shaken until they solidified to the consistency of ice cream.

After lunch, Aunt Akhtar announced that the family drivers would take us on an excursion to a small river-bank called Harro, a tributary of the Indus. We spent a large part of the afternoon and early evening playing on the sandy banks and wading into the shallow water. Large boulders sat in the water, which we used in games of territorial combat, as there were more boys than girls in the group. One boulder sat at a distance from the others and had been seized as a fort by my brother and two other male cousins. They prevented any of us from either climbing up or dragging them down and mounted a defence by hurling chunks of mud-covered moss at us. Another group launched a savage water fight, trying to make the boys slip off the rock.

Onshore, the drivers of both cars, seeing that a massive wave was rolling toward us, shouted at us to return, but it was difficult to make out what they were saying. We continued to ignore them until a crest of advancing water appeared on the horizon, leading us to make a frantic and terrifying dash for the shore. Safely ashore and racing to the cars, we knew that if our parents learned that we had disregarded the drivers, we would not be allowed to venture out to the river again. The drivers were sworn to secrecy by the wiles of the prettiest cousin, who shed tears so her beautiful eyes trembled in anguish. We also shelved the plan to stop for a mouth-watering roadside snack of *chaat,* a chickpea and potato concoction swimming in tamarind and garnished with onions and coriander.

Returning to my uncle's house, we entered the central courtyard. Here, the flooding river paled in comparison to the disturbance amid the household's preparations for the special dinner. All ears were tuned to the commotion emerging from the storeroom, a sublevel room stocked with sacks of basmati rice, flour, lentils, homemade pickles, sweet preserves, exotic cashew and pine nuts, valuable spices, including saffron and black cumin, and mounds of spare crockery. Uncle Bashir, armed with one of his ever-present notebooks, was apparently conducting a food inventory and had discovered that the prized aged basmati rice grown on family land was missing. It had, in fact, been replaced by an inferior rice. His investigation, conducted in thunderous tones, reverberated through the house. The fragrant long-grain rice, traditionally aged to enhance the flavour, was the cornerstone of any Kashmiri household's grain stock. This was the rice that was to be served at dinner.

While the fragrance of spices permeated the house, romance was instantly shadowed by the possibility that the favoured sous-chef of the house had conducted a daring theft. His instant dismissal would be the result. Uncle Bashir, wreathed in scarves and a long formal coat, led the suspect to his study. Pandemonium broke loose in the kitchen. Akhtar, her nose diamond flashing, sliced through four shoulders of lamb and spat out a spirited defence of her missing assistant. My mother and aunts tried to hush her, as they knew their brother's temper, and any act countermining his authority would create more havoc. Then another significant culinary problem reared its head. No one was certain if the small turnips had been pricked and salted in advance, for the person responsible for preparing them was being interrogated. The possibility of changing the menu was discussed, but the curly-haired suitor had been promised a Kashmiri delicacy, and the delights of anticipation could not be thwarted.

Uncle Bashir was a just man. He booked a series of trunk calls, the term we used for long distance calls in those days, to the overseer of the rice-growing property to determine if the wrong bag of rice had been shipped to him. Somewhere inside his just heart also flourished a flair for crisis management. The dinner to be served that night would be complemented by fresh chapatis, arriving to the dinner table one at a time as they were cooked, and the suspect under interrogation had a skill for making them that was quite unrivalled. The dinner, decided my uncle, could not be jeopardized, and so he would postpone the dismissal, if it came to that, until the next day. After all, the family was known not only for the beauty of its women and love of poetry, but also by what was served on the table. My uncle made arrangements to borrow some rice from a friend, as it was obvious the telephone exchange operator intended to sleep on the job, and the suspect was ordered to resume his kitchen duties.

Aunt Dilara's suitor arrived with a wreath of jasmine for the object of his desire and boxes of sweets for the gathering. Dinner was a stately affair in the long dining room. The scent of cinnamon and saffron rose from the tureens of shebdeg. Tender chunks of lamb shoulder and young turnips swam in a golden-brown sauce and were cheerfully ladled over second-grade basmati rice. It was a culinary travesty in my uncle's mind, but one overlooked by the guest of honour because my aunt Dilara, wearing jasmine in her hair and a glow on her face, was seated across from him.

Conversation of menus served for wedding feasts flowed across the dining table. The bridegroom-to-be appeared knocked senseless by his fiancée, the food and the ponderous solemnity of my uncle's bulky form. My mother and aunts beamed and rustled their pastel silks as they leaned forward to converse, their five different perfumes battling with the aroma of the food. Goaded by forces larger than himself, the suitor promptly finalized the date for the wedding. At this point, Uncle Bashir informed him that it all depended on the availability of his younger brother, the magical Amir, who often volunteered to supervise the chefs hired for family weddings. A collective thrill shot down the dining table. Any reason for having the fabled, elusive Amir in our midst was cause for celebration. Secretly, we wondered if the bridegroom-to-be knew that his true mettle would be tested by Amir's chili paste, not by the jewellery he bought for his wife.

All night long my uncle pulled culinary aces from his sleeve until the incorrigible Aunt Akhtar sent for the dessert, which had been prepared not at home but at a local sweet shop. As far she was concerned, the uproar created by the missing rice and the preparation of the turnips and lamb had left no time to make anything at home. My uncle's glacial disapproval and a platter of commercially made *jalebis*, transparent coils of deep-fried batter soaked in honey syrup, landed on the table simultaneously. This dessert, symbolic of romantic courtship, was eaten only with the fingers. When my aunt Dilara was coaxed by Aunt Akhtar to lift one in her fingertips and place it in her curly-haired suitor's mouth, the chill descending from my uncle lifted.

❧

Kashmiri shebdeg—turnips and lamb—became a dish linked to my uncle and his wife. It was often prepared superbly in my mother's kitchen, but what was served with it that night at my uncle's home was an accompanying dish called ambience. The sizzle of battling temperaments, the taste of romance and the bouquet of a close-knit family made this dish sit apart from others. Many years later, I learned to cook it after several frustrating attempts.

Before he died, Uncle Bashir came to Boston to visit a pair of dazzling Kashmiri cooks, his son and daughter-in-law, who managed the dining services of Harvard

University. I considered this a Mughal coup of significant proportions and hoped they would slip a Kashmiri dish into their menus.

During that visit, I took my uncle for a drive in my little convertible with the hood down. He immediately donned a baseball cap and stated that he would like to eat an American hamburger. As he sat eating his hamburger with remarkable enthusiasm in the passenger seat, he told me that the maple was the tree of Kashmir and the maple leaf appeared in every Kashmiri decorative motif. He wondered whether this had influenced my decision to choose Canada as my new homeland. We discussed the coincidence at length, and then I offered to take him for an American dessert. He refused, saying that he had to be careful about his diet, and in fact the only desserts that interested him were those my mother made. Had I learned to make any of them?

Kashmiri Turnips and Lamb (*Shebdeg*)

This recipe can be doubled but should not be halved. Shebdeg leftovers taste better the next day. Choose accompanying dishes carefully. Grilled kebabs or leafy spinach greens are a good choice, but starchy vegetables such as potatoes and gourds will detract from the turnip.

1/4 cup plus 3 tablespoons vegetable oil

1 pound small white turnips, peeled, pricked with a
    fork and salted

3 medium onions, thinly sliced

4 1/2 cups water

2 pounds lamb (ribs or shoulder)

2 cloves garlic, ground to a paste

2-inch piece ginger, ground to a paste

1-inch-long cinnamon stick

2 tablespoons coriander powder

1 teaspoon black cumin seeds

1/2 teaspoon red chilies

1/2 teaspoon saffron, crushed and soaked in 1/4 cup
    warm water

2 teaspoons sugar

1 teaspoon garam masala

1 small bunch fresh coriander, leaves plucked and
    chopped

Coat a skillet with 3 tablespoons of the vegetable oil
and fry the turnips until golden brown. Set aside. Heat
the remaining 1/4 cup oil in a heavy, deep pot and fry
the onions until dark brown and caramelized. Pour in
1/2 cup of the water and cook, mashing the onions with
a heavy spoon, until the liquid is reduced to a third.
Add the lamb, garlic, ginger, cinnamon stick, coriander
powder, cumin and chilies. Stir well so the meat is coated
evenly with the spices, and brown over medium heat.
Add the turnips and enough water to cover the meat,
about 4 cups.

When the meat is two-thirds done, add the saffron with its soaking water and the sugar. Reduce the heat to low, cover and simmer until the meat is tender. If the turnips are cooked before the meat, remove them carefully and set aside to add to the meat when it is fully cooked. Sprinkle in the garam masala, cover and simmer another 2 minutes, until the garam masala dissolves. Garnish with fresh coriander. Serve with plain steamed rice.

Serves 6.

10

The Siren Song of My Mother's Gajrela

AND IF THE WINE YOU DRINK, THE LIP YOU PRESS,
END IN WHAT ALL BEGINS AND ENDS IN—YES;
THINK THEN YOU ARE TO-DAY WHAT YESTERDAY
YOU WERE—TOMORROW YOU SHALL NOT BE LESS.
—Omar Khayyam, *The Rubaiyat*

✥

Yellow melons, a favourite seasonal fruit of my parents, appeared annually in our Karachi home. My father would split the sarda melon in half with one long stroke of a serrated knife, exposing white flesh and a clump of brown seeds while filling me with disgust. I would have much rather kicked it across the length of the front lawn like a rugby ball. My parents paid unfathomable reverence to the sarda melon, babbling about its arrival from a province called Baluchistan in western Pakistan, and extolling to the point of absurdity its cooling properties and the one mysterious knock on its side that would determine whether it was sweet. The sarda had an outer rind as impenetrable as the hide of a rhinoceros, and the hard white flesh inside, sweet or otherwise, held no appeal for me whatsoever. Eating it was a form of drudgery.

However, I could not express the savage thoughts evoked by this fruit masquerading as a dessert at the dinner table. Both of my parents were firmly ensconced in sarda mania and had moved to that alien zone where parents became totally unrecognizable. The first stirrings of a teenaged revolt against my mother's penchant for serving fruit instead of one of her magnificent desserts took seed in my heart. Although I was certain I could express an opinion about food in some parody of adult sophistication, ultimately I lacked the courage to say that the wonderful dinner was like a story that began with great promise and floundered with an abysmal ending.

My father began to slice the melon, and my mother arranged the slices on a platter to be passed around the table. My father acted as though he were carving some prized delicacy. It was easier to forgive him, as I knew he had entered the kitchen only twice in his lifetime, and even then just to do a quick public relations tour. However, the act of cutting the sarda tied him to my mother. Betrayal, as far as I was concerned, came from both household gods.

Melons had a history in Pakistan that began in the Harrapan civilization of 1500 B.C. This civilization flourished along the Indus River and was both urban and mercantile, trading with Mesopotamia, south India, Afghanistan and Persia. The Harrapans adopted the Mesopotamian model of irrigated agricultural lands, successfully cultivating melons, among other crops. The dispersal of this civilization a hundred years later to the northeastern part of the country remains an archaeological mystery. One logical assumption is that the people left in search of more fertile land as a result of topsoil erosion, depletion of nutrients from the soil or even a change in the course of the Indus River.

The fruit basket of Pakistan is Baluchistan and its capital city of Quetta, which lies at the mouth of the Bolan Pass, ringed by a range of coppery red mountains. Melons, grapes, cherries, peaches and plums are grown in the area. From the city of Chaman, which means "garden," there is a direct link to neighbouring Afghanistan, and the southern tip borders Iran. The melon, which grew in these regions, interested the Mughals because it was a hardy fruit that could withstand transportation and yielded enough sugar, fibre and juice to make up an entire meal. The Persians used melons in sherbets and fruit juices and even chilled them. Sarda melons also travelled from China through the Silk Route.

Despite this illustrious history, I felt that the dreaded sarda melon, a cultivated hybrid, had succeeded in rudely nudging aside the fragrant cantaloupe, honeydew and watermelon simply because my parents wished to sabotage the comfort of familiar and predictable food. Ironically, with enough exposure, the unusual and even the unwanted became the familiar, as was the case with the buffalo milk I drank for breakfast as a child. Nevertheless, I continued to reject the sarda.

In my parents' Kashmiri household, fruit was served at the end of a meal. My mother's desserts were matchless but reserved for special occasions, such as visits from guests, specific celebrations and Muslim festivals. A digestive green tea would appear in place of dessert. In a perfect world, I saw rice puddings in clay pots, carrot puddings in deep bowls, carrot halwa studded with almonds and raisins cooked in ghee, and balls of cottage cheese cooked in fragrant cream or soaked in rose-scented sugar syrups appearing magically at the end of every meal. My mother, on the other hand, had created a mystique around dessert and believed it could not be served with every meal. Life had to deliver moments when a food could be celebratory, symbolic or even political. Secretly, I wondered as an adult if a historical tradition was responsible for her inflexibility.

During the reign of the Mughal emperor Humanyun, the Hindu queen Karnawati, rani of Chitor, was under attack from the king of Gujrat. The queen sent the emperor a *rakhi* and sweets. In this Hindu custom, called *raksha bandhan,* a sister tied a silk thread, or rakhi, around

her brother's wrist and presented sweets to him to celebrate
a brother's love and protection of his sister. The rani of
Chitor had made this gesture, pronouncing the emperor
a brother, in the hopes of securing his protection. The
emperor, realizing this significance, set out immediately
to protect the Hindu queen. Sweetening the palate was
essential because it sweetened the disposition as well.
Had the romance of Mughal traditions led my mother to
make her children pine for dessert, so that when it
appeared, the weight of anticipation would transform
it into magical food?

Whenever my mother prepared my favourite dessert,
gajrela, in my childhood, I was prompted to top my
brother's score in the annals of crime committed in
the pantry. On one occasion, the night before the
annual feast marking the end of Ramadan, my mother,
as was customary, had spent all evening in the kitchen
preparing desserts. Various types of vermicelli dishes
and rice puddings would have sufficed, as the stream
of visitors to the house would come bearing boxes of
sweets, yet on this instance, my mother's Kashmiri
streak asserted itself and she included an additional
dessert. Gajrela is a creamy concoction of shredded
carrots, cardamom, saffron, almonds and milk, cooked
to a delicate coral cream. This dish induced a numbing
gluttony in me as well as the extended family, and
records of its consumption were both mind-boggling

and true. I called it my mother's secret weapon, and it took me years to match her skill in preparing it.

Late that night, the mighty gajrela resting in a deep bowl in the refrigerator sent a siren song wafting from the pantry to my bedroom. I decided to dump my brother and conduct a solo midnight raid. In the darkened pantry, I opened the refrigerator and gazed for an eternity at the blue bowl covered with edible silver foil. I knew that the foil, stretched to the edges of the bowl, would part immediately if I dipped in a spoon. I shut and opened the refrigerator door, weighing my options. Did I have the courage to endure my mother's displeasure on a feast day? In a burst of recklessness, I slid a fork along the edges of the bowl, reducing the circumference of the foil and creating a channel where I could scoop up the dessert. Each mouthful sliding down my throat was flavoured with the most exquisite guilt. I knew then that the seduction of my palate was so complete that it would make me completely oblivious to any draconian punishment levelled my way. Omar Khayyam's words rang in my ears: "Heaven but a Vision of fulfill'd Desire, / And Hell the Shadow from a Soul on fire."

❧

As an adolescent, I was convinced my mother's desserts could perform miracles. A tower of palm-sized clay bowls appeared in our pantry a couple of times a year, travelling in straw baskets from some mysterious destination. Each bowl was wrapped in newspaper and surrounded in mounds of dust. As I learned later, they were skimmed off pottery wheels and fired in wood-burning kilns. These unglazed pots were pure terracotta, often with uneven edges. The life and thoughts of the potter at work would emerge as thumbprints. Even the thickness of the clay varied, yet none of these details robbed them of their primitive charm.

The clay pots were soaked in cold water overnight and then dried. My mother's elegant *firni*, a rice-powder and cream pudding, was set in these bowls, which were then covered with *varak*, edible silver foil, and garnished with finely slivered pistachios. Even at a formal dining table, the clay bowls filled with dessert altered the ambience of the occasion. An instant connection to the organic self arose, and all nostalgic yearning for cultural roots was temporarily suspended. The indigenous serving bowls, costing less than ten cents apiece, made fine china or precious metals pale in comparison. The clay kept the contents cool and over time sucked the moisture out of the milk, reducing the dessert to a thicker, creamier consistency.

My mother made firni in vast quantities, for she was not content to serve it only to her own family. The Kashmiri tendency to derive joy from feeding others raged excessively in my mother's heart.

At the age of thirteen and fourteen respectively, I and my brother were instructed by a tutor once a week in reading the Koran. The sacred scripture of the Muslim faith was written in Arabic, and although translations in many languages existed, spiritual convention dictated that Arabic had to be mastered to read the Koran in its authentic text. The lessons were never cancelled, and our mother monitored our progress by appearing for sudden spot checks. I disliked the tutor intensely, for he was a dismissive and acerbic man. There was a stultifying formality to the session; we had to show great respect for the teacher and could never question his method of instruction. When he rode up on his bicycle, a prickle of fear invaded my sunny childhood.

My brother handled the situation with his inimitable delinquency, making lengthy visits to the bathroom in the middle of the hour-long sessions. For some reason this failed to disturb the tutor, and I was left to struggle alone. Every error I made was registered with an icy glance of disapproval, signifying that I had committed an act of sacrilege. This excruciating burden was relieved on one occasion when the tea tray was sent up. Each session the tutor, who appeared to have a raging appetite, consumed a plate of savoury and sweet snacks with a potful of tea, as we stumbled through Arabic script. However, on this occasion, three clay bowls filled with firni sat on the tea tray. I was outraged by my mother's generosity to a person

I considered my tormentor. As far as I was concerned, a cup of hemlock would have been sufficient.

The tutor scraped the first bowl with the edge of his spoon and placed dollops of firni in his mouth. The rosewater scenting the dish wafted across the table. I recited lines of text, eyelids fluttering nervously and casting glances upward at my tutor. As he finished his second bowl, the ferocity in his pupils seemed diminished, beads of perspiration dotted his upper lip and even his posture relaxed. At the end of the third bowl, I heard the phrase "Shukr-al-hamdu-lillah," which meant "thanks to God" in Arabic, intoned by the tutor in a throaty, passionate voice. This was followed by a miracle. He offered me my first smile ever, and even assisted with a tip to link the script together. Three months later, I recited verses of the Koran with immaculate articulation at a family celebration, where I received my first piece of serious jewellery and polished off bowls of firni.

❦

Later in life, I chose a safer path. My brilliant mother had woven a formidable mystique around her desserts. Like her, I served fruit at the end of dinner but remained too intimidated to make firni in my Canadian kitchen. Instead, I made chocolate soufflés and caramelized crème brûlées with practised efficiency when I had to. I believed that my Kashmiri heritage, with all its glorious Mughal underpinnings, would be enshrined in a memory of a dessert I was incapable of resurrecting in my Canadian home.

After my father died, I was consumed by painful reveries. I felt as though one of my long-distant moorings had slipped away. Then one morning, the day before the feast of Ramadan, I was overcome by memories of my father on this feast day. I telephoned my mother in Pakistan and casually inquired about the ingredients in firni. After giving me the details, she ended the conversation by saying, "You have to keep stirring it constantly so it never sticks to the bottom, for even if a spoonful burns it will destroy the taste."

I drove immediately to a street in Toronto lined with South Asian grocery stores. It was a Mughal quest of sorts. The route through the tall buildings in the city was like a pass in the Hindu Kush Mountains. My little car was like a Mongolian pony racing to invade India. To go through dozens of grocery stores browsing for clay pots required the stamina of Afghans. To convince the Indian store owner that I wished to purchase his entire stock of small, unglazed clay pots, I summoned Persian diplomacy. He informed me that the clay pots were used as oil lamps during the Hindu festival of lights, and asked me if I planned to set my house on fire. I told him I was a Kashmiri Mughal skilled at both invasion and assimilation.

As with all small miracles, not only did I duplicate my mother's firni perfectly, but my guests thought the clay bowl presentation was the most engaging table decor they had ever seen. Unlike my family in Pakistan, who disposed of the bowls since they were so readily available, I carefully cleaned mine and stored them in my kitchen cupboard. I also wanted to serve the firni to a friend who could not attend my dinner party. The next day, I delivered two bowls to her home, and she uttered a comment that intrigued me, as I knew that exquisite wisdom often lay behind her quietly expressed words. We stood close and she held the two clay bowls in her hand. As she peered through the transparent wrap at the edible silver foil, garnished with slivers of pistachio, she commented that I should write a book about food. I had no way of knowing at that point that she had in fact envisioned my culinary dreamscape.

&

The members of my Kashmiri family taught me that creating ambience, whether by design or accident, becomes part of the food itself, and we begin to store images, in a sort of memory food bank. Unlike firni, which formed one central image for me, I stored many images of gajrela, carrot pudding. One particular memory linked it to the mysteries of the sea.

My childhood home of Karachi was a seaport jutting into the Arabian Sea. In A.D. 712, the Arabs, led by Mohammad Bin Qasim, landed close to Karachi and ruled the region for about two hundred years. The name Karachi evolved from its reputation as a fishing village that offered only *kara machi,* or ocean fish.

We spent most weekends at the beach home of my parents' closest friends. The children were of similar ages, and both our mothers had attended the same universities. The association of our mutual grandparents went to a time before Partition. Their grandfather was the first governor general of the new nation of Pakistan, while ours gave birth to a group of Kashmiri rebels who would serve this nation in unique and distinguished ways. I remember visiting and playing in the gilded interior of the official residence and being served lunch by liveried staff, who arranged formal printed menus on the table for lunch. Yet it was at the beach house where offerings from the sea and the table left a series of unforgettable memories.

It was an hour's drive through the bustling city of Karachi on a Friday afternoon to the home perched on a high cliff, overlooking the glistening waters of the Arabian Sea. Hampers of fruit and salad vegetables, coolers of cooked food and wooden racks filled with bottled Coca-Cola and a local maroon drink called Vimto, made gaseous to dangerous proportions, filled the trunks of the cars. Drinking a couple bottles of Vimto was like becoming a helium balloon on the verge of an explosion.

The beach house was built of grey concrete and studded with shuttered windows that looked out to the ocean. The interior was designed so that bedrooms lined up on one side and the eating and lounging space on the other. The house was equipped with comforts such as a power generator in a small adjoining room, which provided electricity for the lights, hot water and the kitchen appliances.

A long staircase of sixty concrete steps led down to the unspoilt private beach, called Balegi. Rock formations extending from the cliff banked the water, creating natural coves. The hazards of avoiding the lethal jellyfish on the beach were compensated by the dolphins, giant sea turtles and red snapper swimming in the ocean. Even the powdered coffee drunk from a flask and the shami kebabs tucked between two slices of bread tasted finer eaten on this beach.

One weekend, my mother's gajrela travelled to Balegi Beach. It was as though the Mughal emperor Akbar had set forth with his favourite musician, Tansen. Mughal folklore insists that when Tansen played the *veena*, a stringed instrument, even rocks wept. He was lured from another patron by the emperor, who sent an envoy carrying valuable elephants and precious jewels. At Tansen's death on April 26, 1589, the emperor broke tradition by ordering all his musicians and singers to compose melodies at the gravesite, as though it were a wedding instead of a funeral.

Each time a camel or a flock of sheep decided to cross Korangi Road, heading for the beach, and the car braked to a sudden halt, I wondered if my mother's legendary dessert would spill over. The gajrela travelled in a deep cooking pot with a covered lid fastened by a square of cloth. The four ends of the cloth met across the top of the lid in a tight knot to ensure that sand would not enter the dessert.

I had seen the coral-tinted cream pudding being poured into the travelling pot, and was confident that within a few hours I would eat bowlfuls of my favourite dessert. I was addicted to all cream-based deserts made with saffron and was hypnotized by the pale coral of gajrela, a delicate contrast to the rainbow-coloured Pakistani sweets and pure white rice puddings.

A full moon blazed that night, turning the sea to a sheet of silver. After the mouth-watering delights of gajrela, we put into action a midnight excursion to the beach, for the giant sea turtles often chose moonlit nights to swim to the beach and lay eggs, which they would then bury in the sand.

After the adults fell asleep, five teenagers armed with a single flashlight headed down the steep staircase to the sea to watch the turtles. As all exciting ventures were celebrated with the accompaniment of food, the gajrela was the only midnight snack worthy of contemplation. The leftover portion, still sitting in the large cooking pot in the refrigerator, was removed and knotted into the same cloth. Five spoons were tucked into a pocket, and within minutes gajrela reached the beach.

When a moving wall of dark objects crawled out of the ocean to the sand, there was a hushed silence. Twenty gigantic sea turtles dug out hollows with their feet, rested on the hollows to deposit mounds of rubbery white eggs and retreated into the sea. Perched on a rock and spooning out gajrela as we watched the scene played out on the sand, both offerings, one from my mother and the other from the sea, shone brighter than the moon.

To me, the saffron-flavoured shredded carrot pudding always brings back sea creatures, moonbeams and the buoyancy of saltwater. Years later, while I was boating in Mexico, a young man swam on the back of a giant sea turtle beside us. His ride was precarious, as the turtle was aware of the boat beside it and swam defensively in a bobbing motion. Watching this enthralling spectacle made me wonder how I could magically summon a bowl of chilled gajrela to offer the rider when he slipped off the turtle.

My first attempt at making gajrela was a disaster. Handicapped with a fair amount of culinary arrogance, I made the mistake of thinking that I could use electrical appliances to shorten the cooking time. The speed with which I cooked made those around me heap compliments on my skill. My North American life was not one of Mughal leisure. I cooked in advance so I could enjoy the company of those who came to dine, rather than being trapped in the kitchen. If a dish had to be prepared at the last minute, I would serve an informal meal in my kitchen. However, this informality never sat well with me. I was raised in a culture where a culinary delight was simply presented but its creation was always designed to be invisible. Surprise was an intriguing component of presenting food. Responses could then be gauged and stored away to customize the dish for a particular person. This type of cooking was an accepted form of displaying love.

On my second attempt at making gajrela, I let it cook longer, allowing the enzymes in the milk to convert the shredded carrot into particles of saffron-tinted cream. I also found a deep blue-glass bowl that would complement the apricot tint of the dessert. The taste of the gajrela was perfect, yet the taste I remembered as a child remained mysteriously elusive, as distant as my mother's home continents away.

❦

One chilly November morning, I sat at a table outside a coffee shop in my neighbourhood. I was drinking an inferior brew of coffee from a disposable cup. The friend to whom I had brought bowls of firni passed by. We chatted for a while, and I felt that she was probing to discover whether the seed she had planted so effortlessly in my mind some time ago was showing any signs of sprouting. Had I thought about writing about food? Later that night, in the outline of a dream, I saw the ghost of a historical pageant, inhaled the fragrance of love and tasted many courses at a meal. Then I realized that love and food was all that was required to spend a day with a Kashmiri family anywhere.

Kashmiri Carrot Pudding (*Gajrela*)

The Gajrela is a sumptuous cream-based dessert. It should be served at the end of a light meal. A bowl of gajrela also makes a superb breakfast or a snack at any time of day.

8 green cardamom pods, crushed to a powder
3 tablespoons ghee or light vegetable oil
I pound carrots, grated
I cup sugar
2 litres milk
I litre table cream (IO percent)
I cup slivered almonds
I/4 cup rice, parboiled
I teaspoon crushed saffron
Edible silver foil, for decorating

In a 4- or 6-quart cooking pot, roast the cardamom powder in the ghee or oil for a few seconds, then add the grated carrot and sugar. Sauté until the sugar melts and the carrots become limp. Stir in the milk, cream, almonds, rice and saffron. Cook over low heat for 2 hours, stirring occasionally to dislodge the cream gathering on the surface and mixing well, until the carrots become soft and creamy and the rice almost disintegrates. Chill the cooked gajrela for about 3 hours. Before serving, cover the surface with edible silver foil.

Serves 6.

Further Reading

Kadri, Justice Syed Shameem Hussain. *Creation of Pakistan*. Lahore: Wajidalis, 1982.

Khan, Pervez A. *Wonders of the Karakorum*. Lahore: Ferozsons, 1996.

Lewis, Bernard (ed.). *The World of Islam, Faith, People, Culture*. New York: Thames and Hudson, 1992.

Quraeshi, Samina. *Lahore: The City Within*. Singapore: Concept Media, 1988.

Tavernier, Jean-Baptiste. *Travels in India*. Translated from original 1676 French edition by V. Ball. London/New York: MacMillan and Co., 1889. Reprint, New Delhi: Munshiram Manoharlal, 1995.